THE BILL FROM THE CHINA SHOP

THE BILL FROM THE
CHINA SHOP

HOW ASIA'S SAVINGS GLUT
THREATENS THE WORLD ECONOMY

Charles Dumas
&
Diana Choyleva

P

PROFILE BOOKS

First published in Great Britain in 2006 by
Profile Books Ltd
3A Exmouth House
Pine Street
London EC1R OJH
www.profilebooks.com

Typeset in Times by MacGuru Ltd
info@macguru.org.uk
Printed and bound in Great Britain by
Bell & Bain Ltd.

A CIP catalogue record for this book is available from the British Library.

ISBN-10 1 86197 871 5
ISBN-13 978 1 86197 871 4

Contents

Figures and tables

Acknowledgements

The specific idea of inverting global imbalances from a US deficit problem to a Eurasian surplus problem was Charles's, but it owed a lot to the *zeitgeist* in 2004, with the dollar growing ever weaker and no sign of any improvement in the US deficit. The growing importance of China was also widely appreciated.

The Chinese yuan–dollar peg was constantly discussed by Brian Reading and ourselves, with Brian contributing much of the structural thinking behind the concept of the New Dollar Area, the quasi-fixed, trans-Pacific currency zone made up of the US, China, Japan and the Asian Tigers. The determined sustenance of Asian surpluses involved in such exchange rate policies was a key factor pointing to structural surpluses, rather than merely investor preferences for US securities, as the fundamental reason for US deficits being so easily financed. Some of these issues had also come up in a presentation by Martin Wolf of the *Financial Times* to the Political Economy Club. The use of sectoral financial balances – analysis of the interactive financial balances and behaviour patterns of households, businesses, the government and the rest of the world – was pioneered by Brian thirty years ago, and has been vital to our approach. Brian also participated in Diana's forecast of a Chinese slowdown, which we expect to be extended in 2006–07. We owe him a lot.

The thought that there should be an actual book came from Frank Veneroso, who played a large part in Lombard Street Research's New York seminar on the Eurasian surpluses and Chinese slowdown, held on 8 March 2005, a fortuitous two days before Ben Bernanke's speech talking of a 'global savings glut'.

Our colleagues in Lombard Street Research have been models of patience as the work on this book has sometimes distracted us from full attention to our duties. Peter Allen, our managing director, has also been instrumental in securing its publication, whipping us on, and helping with editing, the title, the cover illustration, and numerous other important aspects of the fact that it is here at all.

Introduction

Most of us are influenced by Mr Micawber's dictum: 'Annual income twenty pounds, annual expenditure nineteen nineteen six, result happiness. Annual income twenty pounds, annual expenditure twenty pounds ought and six, result misery.' Translation: deficits are bad, surpluses are good. It is a natural viewpoint that the purpose of politics and policy is to put right wrongs. So, even if we cannot create happiness, let us at least attack misery! Away, deficits and borrowing!

We are also in the habit of regarding the United States as active, others as reactive. America has the largest and most persistent deficits. So US deficits are the cause of the global financial imbalances. Right?

Wrong!

The world has an Asian current-account surplus problem rather than a US current-account deficit problem. The complex effects of this surplus have been central to our analysis of the world economy since mid-2004 and underpin the argument of this book. After five or six years of accepting consensus views about the 'unsustainable' US deficit(s), the fact that they were nevertheless sustained began to force a rethink. Hence the idea that they are not some peculiar perversion, but are derived from something more fundamental and structural – an effect, not a cause. In March 2005, Ben Bernanke, successor to Alan Greenspan as chairman of the Federal Reserve, followed the same logic, attributing US financial deficits to an 'Asian savings glut'. For the Fed, his argument is convenient almost to the point of being self-serving. But it seems right.[1]

This book sets out the concept of the Eurasian savings excess as a structural rather than cyclical phenomenon. Although north-central Europe has a large portion of the Eurasian structural surplus, by late 2005 it was almost entirely offset by deficits elsewhere in Europe. So the story breaks down into an intra-European imbalance and a global imbalance, the latter almost entirely driven by the Asian savings glut, which is therefore the phrase mostly used here. It describes the 'perfect storm' comprising four largely unrelated forces, and the countries to which they variously apply. It examines how the start of this structural surplus manifested itself in the US 1998–2000 bubble.

The alternative responses by policymakers and the private sector are outlined. The surplus tends to inflate asset prices, but not consumer prices – the 'Goldilocks' economy – so long as global demand is sustained by deficit policies. The post-bubble recovery in 2002–05 is shown to depend on spectacularly easy fiscal and monetary policies, and the consequent build-up of household debt; both of these in any other circumstances would quickly have caused major inflation. The new dollar area with its semi-fixed exchange rates has been a key transmission mechanism for the Asian glut. This is based on the Chinese yuan–dollar peg: other Asian countries have managed their exchange rates in order to match the yuan out of fear of being 'hollowed out' by China's burgeoning manufacturing prowess. After a look at the long-term damage from savings excesses in Japan (1990–2003) Part I of the book concludes with the stresses that threaten this Sino-US synergy of lending and borrowing, and hence global growth. A severe trans-Pacific crisis is forecast for 2007.

The second part of the book looks in greater detail at China, whose economic developments have been central to the Asian savings glut story. China is the largest-ever developing economy in transition from command to market. Its under-developed financial system and the interaction between rigid politics and liberal economics have created a unique economic structure, prone to violent cyclical swings. Leaving the huge domestic savings in the hands of state banks, which lend mainly to the state firms without being governed by market principles, results in massive overinvestment with little regard for return on capital. Policy tightening and overheating have restrained runaway domestic demand growth since mid-2004. But exports continue to power ahead, resulting in a ballooning current account surplus. The start of the work-out of China's domestic imbalances marks the beginning of the end of the NDA. The severe crisis we are forecasting for 2007 will be the decisive test of the Chinese authorities' resolve to push ahead with the painful structural reforms needed, if China is to remain on a sustainable strong long-term growth path.

PART I

CHARLES DUMAS

1

Typhoon surplus

Economics is a combination of, and a balancing act between, science and art. Scientific propositions such as Newton's Third Law of Motion – 'To every action there is an equal and opposite reaction' – have their counterparts. For every borrower there is a lender, and vice versa. At the macro-level, for every deficit there is a surplus, and vice versa. These two propositions are closer to being self-evident than even Newton's Third Law. The art of economics, by contrast, comes in the many instances where judgement is required, as well as an understanding of laws and theory. An example is deciding, in the case of borrowing and lending, which is the cause and which is the effect, assuming this can be done. (Interactive cause and effect is also often observed.) In monetary theory, it is usual to see borrowing as the action and lending as the reaction. In a closed economy (one with no external sector, neither foreign trade nor capital flows) to have it the other way round would be strange. But it is not conceptually impossible.

Although the world as a whole is a closed economy, individual countries are not. But we are accustomed to see deficits (borrowing)

Figure 1 **Current account balances**
$ billion

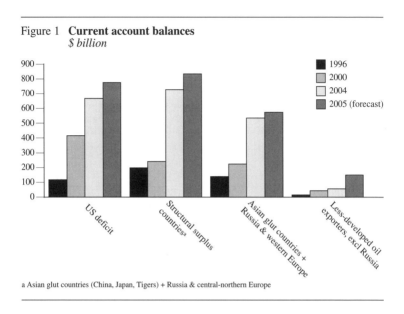

a Asian glut countries (China, Japan, Tigers) + Russia & central-northern Europe

as the action, and the equal and opposite surpluses (lending) as the reaction. This is true both between open economies in the world at large, and within economies (closed or open) between borrowers and lenders.

This book is intended to expose these misconceptions. It is the Asian current-account surpluses that are the fundamental driver, as large and chronic surpluses in central-northern Europe are to a great degree offset by deficits elsewhere within Europe. The US deficit is the reaction – not so much profligate extravagance, but the result of pursuing full-employment/low-inflation policies in a world full of countries determined to run surpluses. This is not an iron-clad, bullet-proof assertion. Elements of fiscal and monetary irresponsibility can be found in US policies over the past five or six years, it must be said, but the broad direction of causation is clear. Asian (and some European) countries run high-savings/current-account surplus economies partly as a matter of policy and partly for deep structural and behavioural reasons. America and to a lesser degree Britain and Australia (and now European countries such as Italy, Spain and increasingly France) have simply adjusted their fiscal and monetary policies to borrow Asia's excess savings. It would be rude to refuse!

In this interpretation of recent events, the one 'problem' that does not exist is the US trade or current deficit (now nearly $800 billion a year). The problem is not for the United States to find $2 billion a day to fund its deficit, as has so often been stated. Rather, the problem is for the Asian, together with some European, countries to find a home for $1.5 billion a day of capital generated by their surpluses. This surplus moves like a tidal wave from balance sheet to balance sheet, between businesses, households and government, loading them with extra debt. It has helped induce undue borrowing by US business (1998–2000), by Australian and British households (1999–2004), by American households (2001–05), by Chinese business (2002–04) and recently by Spain and increasingly Italy.

Asia's decisive shift into current-account surplus came after the 1997–98 Asian crisis. Initially, the surplus typhoon strongly reinforced the Wall Street bubble of 1998–2000; then it drove the British and Australian debt-fuelled housing booms of 1999–2004. Both countries developed large, easily financed deficits during this period. American households followed suit from late 2001, and Asian surpluses were recycled back into a Chinese boom in 2002–04. To this private-sector debt stimulation must be added acceptance in the United States, Europe and Japan of government deficits far beyond what is generally regarded as prudent – especially in the context of looming pension financing problems in most of these countries. The exhaustion of borrowing power in private-sector balance sheets is now increasingly likely – and soon – after which persistent Asian surpluses are likely to cause a general global deflation. Government deficits worldwide will further expand. How governments handle their fast-growing indebtedness to surplus nations alongside financing baby-boomers' pensions will be the western nations' economic challenge of the next 5–10 years.

What does 'excessive saving' mean?

Current-account surpluses represent the excess of a country's domestic savings over its investment. Globally, they must be matched by deficits elsewhere (though in practice because of measurement errors there is always a trivial difference). Put another way, the world's saving and investment have to be equal. Saving equals income minus consumption, government plus household. Investment equals output, i.e. GDP, which should equal income minus the part consumed. So saving equals investment by definition. But if the desire to invest is less than the desire to save, demand will fall short: unwanted investment in the form of stock – inventory – will occur, leading to a downward economic spiral if no other factor intervenes. (See Chapter 2 for other possible

Table 1 **Swing in US and European budget deficits after the bubble**

| | Government balance (% GDP) | | Difference | |
	2000	2004	%	$ billion
US	1.6	–4.3	–5.9	690
Euro zone	0.1	–2.7	–2.8	270
UK	1.6	–3.4	–5.0	110
Total	1.0	–3.6	–4.6	1,070

Note. Japan's deficit was already 7.5% of GDP by 2000, as its problems dated from earlier; a small improvement to 6.1% in 2004 was offset by Scandinavian worsening.

consequences of an excessive desire to save.) The idea proposed here of excessive Asian surpluses implies a global propensity to save that is greater than investment, unless lower interest rates or fiscal policy respond.

To reconcile this apparent contradiction in the concept of a savings glut is not difficult. First, recent years have seen a major growth in deficit countries – and some surplus countries – deliberately dis-saving by running government deficits. This offsets the rising structural saving in the surplus countries' private sectors (Japan and north-central Europe) and in developing countries in Asia. Second, what would threaten to be saving in excess of investment may induce more investment through the operation of depressed real rates of return. Initially, this means lower real bond yields. But as the 'wall of money' drives up stock and real estate prices, another result is lower earnings yields in stockmarkets (i.e. higher price/earnings ratios). Likewise rising property prices

Figure 2 **Overnight interbank money market rates**
%

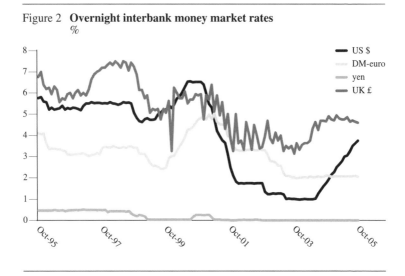

mean lower rental yields in real estate (with high capitalisation ratios).

So far, the primary effect of these lower real yields (apart from making existing wealth-holders much more wealthy) has not been to induce lower-return capital spending, except in the initial case of the US bubble and the more recent 2003–04 Chinese investment boom. Rather, deficit countries have induced lower household savings by easy monetary policies, in parallel with the government dis-saving from easy fiscal policies. The UK, Australian and US 'borrow-and-spend' household spending orgies of the past few years are the first result, reflecting easy monetary and fiscal policies, and easy access to excess Asian saving.

This aggressive cut in government and household saving has substantially exceeded the structural Asian and central-northern

Europe excess savings, and world savings have gone down a little. IMF calculations of world savings put them at 21.5% of the world's $40 trillion GDP in 2004, compared with 22% in 2000. So in four years, in which US-European government deficits rose by $1.1 trillion and US household deficits by a further $250 billion, the global savings rate fell by $200 billion or so (0.5% of $40 billion). This graphically shows the force of burgeoning savings. The chief danger from current-account deficits, most of all in America, arises from these internal cuts in savings, which are achieved by running up debt, rather than from external debt and deficit financing.

It is one thing to assert that America has no problem attracting $2 billion a day of capital inflows. It is quite another to contemplate the point that its recently depressed national savings rate of 14% of GDP will in due course have to be raised. The difference between this and the national investment rate of 20% of GDP mirrors the current-account deficit, which is 6–6.5% of GDP. Not only is investment only 60% covered by saving, but domestic demand is over 106% of GDP. As US GDP is close to its potential, this gap can only be narrowed – if it is to be narrowed – by cuts in domestic demand. Although the structural nature of the Asian surpluses means this problem will probably not be forced to resolution by US creditors, the time of reckoning will come – soon if the argument in the last section of this book is correct. But American consumers undoubtedly regard this overconsumption as their entitlement. When the punch-bowl is taken away, the end of the party, and the relapse into hangover, could prove ugly.

Another, deeper, aspect of this excess of savings is the wasted

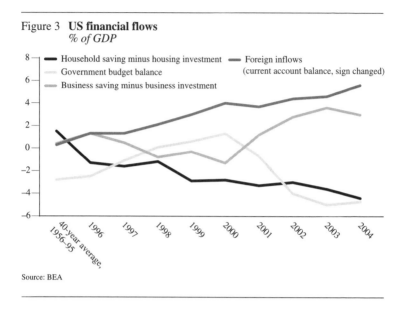

Figure 3 **US financial flows**
         % of GDP

Source: BEA

opportunity it represents. One way to look at the world economy today is to say that a relatively balanced OECD economy in the late 1980s – with capital and labour reasonably in proportion to one another – has been destabilised by entry of the former Soviet bloc and, more importantly, some 1.25 billion Chinese and 1 billion Indians. Among other effects, the bargaining power of western labour is reduced, alongside the capital assets per potential worker. This has been tough on low-income labour in rich countries. It has also underpinned the huge gains in value of existing capital assets (stocks and real estate). High-income labour as well as wealth-holders in rich countries have benefited from these gains.

One result should be a massive investment boom in response to such high returns on assets – a boom that would provide China,

India and eastern European countries with capital assets, transferring technology and raising their average incomes. To some extent this has happened. But major blockages have slowed development – which is tragic, because but for these blockages there would be plenty of highly profitable usages for all the savings the world could muster, and no Asian savings glut. Western countries and governments would not need to induce deficits to dissipate these savings in 'borrow-and-spend'.

The obstructions to adequate growth in the former Soviet bloc are too complex to detail here (and at their worst in eastern Germany). In China, the government's control of both the energy sector (with price controls as well) and the financial sector, and fundamental conditions in the housing sector, together with general problems of corruption and the rule of law, severely hobble growth. Impressive though it is with an annual trend of 8–9%, it should be 11–12%. India, as well as being restricted by appalling infrastructure, has restrictive labour laws that hold back the manufacturing sector and many services. These have ensured that the country with the poorest workers on earth has extremely capital-intensive rather than labour-intensive growth. Ten-year average GDP growth has accelerated to 6.25%, but it should (given other factors) be close to 10%.[2]

The Asian savings glut

A key point is that Asian excess savings are structural, not cyclical. This analysis does not draw conclusions from the essentially cyclical OPEC and Canadian surpluses, which could dissipate quite quickly through some combination of oil prices falling, rapid increases in imports, or (especially for Canada) real exchange rate rises. Better trade balances in Latin America and elsewhere, based on the strength of the global economy (and helped by hefty devaluations quite recently), are likewise not the issue. The contention that US current-account deficits are largely the result of Asian surpluses can only justify sustained fiscal and monetary ease if those surpluses are regarded as structural for the medium term.

Different forces in different countries lead to this common result of persistent current-account surpluses. In China and the Asian Tigers (South Korea, Taiwan, Hong Kong, Thailand, Malaysia, Singapore and Indonesia), development strategy and policy are crucial. Export-led development, the Asian approach, naturally tends to lead to exports surpluses, though they are not inevitable. In developing Asia, where strong exports are buttressed by high savings, a surplus is likely. Moreover, although it is effective to focus development policy on exports, that leaves the domestic financial system crudely devoted to industry, and undeveloped in provision for household needs. This results in high savings rates as financial products for house purchase (mortgages), health and pension provision (insurance and fund management) are neglected. The absence of public social security as well as sophisticated private financial products requires people to save much more to take care of basic realities: losing your job or your health, getting old, buying a house, and so on.

Savings in an economy can be made by households (easily

understood, if complex statistically) or by business, with government budget balances also affecting the overall national savings rate. Business savings are its cash flow matching depreciation (of existing equipment) plus the retained profit that remains after paying interest, taxes and dividends. The structural excess saving in the developed world arises partly from business 'restructuring' – saving much more than is needed for capital spending. The other chief driving force is demography: declining working-age (and increasingly total) populations need less construction investment in particular, as existing factories and offices are sufficient. Large pre-retirement populations can also mean high personal savings rates, as people anticipate post-retirement financial needs. In Japan, business-sector restructuring now predominates as the source of high private-sector saving. But 10–15 years ago excessive Japanese saving was chiefly the result of demography, which remains important. In Germany, Benelux, Scandinavia and Switzerland ('north-central Europe') demography has predominated, but business restructuring is increasingly a factor.

Business restructuring (leading to financial surpluses) has also been significant in the US since the bubble burst in 2000. In overall terms, financial flows must add up to zero – as we saw, each surplus must correspond to somebody else's deficit, and vice versa. So to the US current-account deficit, also known as foreigners' surplus, must be added a business surplus. Only the government and households remain to run the corresponding deficits. So the US business surpluses mean these balancing domestic government and household deficits are even larger than the external deficit that matches other countries' surpluses.

In a global sense, the saving glut is a good example of that fashionable concept, the 'perfect storm'. The mercantilist, market-predatory, export-led policies of Asian developing countries may have greater impact relative to world GDP than similar behaviour in the heyday of Japan (1960s) or South Korea (1970s). But by themselves they could probably be accommodated, along with the structural tendency towards high household savings in countries pursuing the Asian growth model. The natural tendency towards financial surplus in the late careers of 'baby-boomers', exaggerated by fears of ageing arising from rapidly growing longevity, ought to be offset by the capital spending requirements of fast growth in America and rapid development in the emerging markets. But the latter is thwarted by domestic development policy weaknesses as well as the Asian export-led, high-savings model.

The possibility of simply expanding business investment to use up the spare capital is quite rightly rejected by western businesses themselves. They have learned the lessons of the US bubble in 1998–2000 and the Japanese bubble of the late 1980s. This reinforces the shift to shareholder value from bureaucratic business waste, originated by fear of Carl Icahn, T. Boone Pickens and the other corporate raiders of the 1980s, financed by Mike Milken's junk bonds. Rather than being taken over and restructured to generate cash flow and pay off a mound of junk debt, US businesses decided to do the job themselves (keeping their own jobs in the process). Restructuring spread round the world (with a lapse in the bubble), and now worldwide business restructuring is the fourth element of this perfect storm of urge to surplus.

China and the Asian Tigers

Strong growth in China and the Asian Tigers, where open-economy, export-led, high-savings policies have been adopted, contrasts starkly with dismal results in Latin America and pre-1980s India, where low savings, capital imports and import-substitution created closed, siege economies. In Latin America, any move into rapid growth naturally gave rise to booming capital spending – inevitably, given major catch-up potential. With feeble domestic savings, such bursts of growth therefore required soaring imports, not just for financial reasons (i.e. lack of domestic savings) but also for lack of competitive domestic capital goods industries (except perhaps construction). Such growth periods were therefore quickly choked off by debt crises as foreign lenders were discouraged by inflation and deficits, soon followed by inability or unwillingness to repay.

The import-substitution, siege-economy mentality also entailed obstacles to foreign direct investment, such as domestic content quotas, dividend restraints, etc. Meanwhile, competitiveness was further thwarted by domestic cliques and cartels carving up the protected local market. And developing a wide range of industries on a small scale to supply the local market means forgoing the economies of scale that can result from focusing on a few well chosen export industries. India remained financially sound, but simply grew consistently too slowly until the 1980s, with similar constraints.

The Pacific Rim countries' mercantilist approach has ensured competitive industries, because of the need to compete in export

Figure 4 **Actual exports plus imports**
% of GDP, divided by predicted ratio based on population

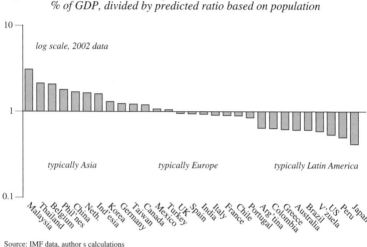

Source: IMF data, author s calculations

markets, and has tended to promote economies of scale. With high savings as well as export focus, capital investment needs, and the imports to supply them, have been easily financed not merely without incurring foreign debt, but with a surplus too. In fact, capital inflows have added to the surplus requiring a 'home' abroad: while the treatment of foreign capital has certainly not been uniformly free-market and transparent, China and others have encouraged direct investment to good effect in achieving rapid technology transfer and job creation.

So far, so good. But Asian fixation on exports and revulsion from deficits became more profound as a result of the inflationary boom-bust of China in 1993–94 and, especially, the Asian crisis of 1997–98. Humiliation was heaped on Asian countries, as their underdeveloped financial systems collapsed under the huge inflows, followed by outflows, of global finance in the 1995–98 boom-bust. This transformed attitudes toward free capital flows. IMF policies towards South Korea and others were clearly driven more by western bank and hedge fund interests than the countries' development needs. 'Never again' has entered the Asian policy vocabulary, in China as much as the countries most affected. The resulting policies – and surpluses – have been and probably will remain persistent.

Japan

The source of surpluses is quite different in Japan. Demographic factors may have held up household savings rates in the 1990s, when the large 1930s generation was in its pre-retirement phase, but now they have retired, personal savings are well below European levels (relative to income) though still well above America's near-zero. It is business that contributes nearly 25 points of Japan's 29% of GDP private-sector savings rate. But private investment needs are less than this by at least 10% of GDP. Here, demographic factors remain important: both the slow growth trend of 2% or less – cutting the need for business investment – and the weakness of house-building have a lot to do with the shrinking working-age population. Private investment is unlikely to raise its share of GDP in future, and could decrease it. So the private sector (unless the economy is to slump) has to run a surplus (be a net lender) of 10% of GDP. Japan's current recovery, including rising house prices for the first time for 15 years, may reduce this surplus over time. Personal savings could be cut by a rundown of huge bank deposits held by some people as a cushion against formerly increasing negative housing equity, and by others as a vehicle for pension provision. As the population ages, having had little or nothing in the late 1940s, it could well consume some of its now large wealth. But such a development is uncertain and likely to be slow.

Once again: for every surplus (lender) there is an equal and opposite deficit (borrower). Apart from the private sector, Japan has only government and foreigners as potential borrowers (i.e. sources of offsetting deficits). For Japan to be close to full employment, government deficits plus current-account surpluses (i.e. foreigners' borrowing) must add up to 10% of GDP. Not surprisingly, it wants as large a current-account surplus as possible to reduce reliance on what is already an alarming build-up of government debt. (In 2004, for example, while the current-account surplus was 3.5% of GDP, the government deficit was 6.5%.) Although the huge 10% private-sector savings surplus should eventually dissipate, businesses still have a way to go to get debt and assets down to stable long-term levels after the excesses of Japan's late-1980s bubble, followed by the delay of business restructuring until 1997 and after. So the country's surplus with the rest of the world is unlikely to ease much in the next three years or so. Japan's private savings of $1.1 trillion are three-quarters of those in the United States, though its economy is less than two-fifths the size. Its excessive savings are a major global force.

Russia

The oligarchs who own much of Russian business effectively stole it in the 1990s. Typically, a new owner, having paid little for business assets in a corrupt privatisation, would generate cash in the company by not paying the wages. The resulting cash would be parked in a Swiss bank account and then transferred into the personal account of the oligarch. So the very process of stealing the money involved capital exports. President Vladimir Putin came to power on a populist wave at least partly because of this. His imprisonment of Mikhail Khodorkovsky, the head of oil giant Yukos, has put the oligarchs on notice. Their natural reactions include continuing to export as much capital as they can (along with their families). Russia's gross savings rate is 31% of GDP, the investment rate is 21%, leaving a current-account surplus of a whopping 10%, some $60 billion.

Russia's chief source of export revenue, as well as oligarchs' wealth, is oil and gas, so the world boom is swelling surpluses in a purely cyclical way. Unlike the structural excess savings, which are inherently linked to a deficiency of demand, cyclical oil-exporting surpluses reflect excess demand, and exacerbate it as the revenues are spent on imports. This concentration of the increased global financial imbalances this year on oil exporters, i.e. cyclical factors reflecting excess demand, is a development that could hasten the debt problems that are likely to end this world boom prematurely. This is discussed more fully in the last section of this book, but it downplays the importance of the Russian surplus in a discussion of a savings glut.

North-central Europe

Germany – and much of north-central Europe – has a large structural surplus, mostly for demographic reasons. Fearful that extravagant state pension promises will be broken, baby-boomers – who have between 6 and 24 years to go before they are 65 – are saving more. In Germany, on the spending side, after five decades of heavy building culminating in the post-reunification boom of 1990–94, a shrinking working-age population means few more (if any) factories or office buildings will ever be needed. The future contraction soon expected for the total population (i.e. not just working-age) may soon make this true of homes too. Yet the construction share of German GDP is still close to that of the United States, despite ten years of shrinkage since the 1994 peak. By now construction should be minimal; its downswing has therefore a lot further to go.

Meanwhile, the recent surge of German business restructuring – i.e. cost-cutting – and the resulting erosion of job security contributes further to households' urge to save, as well as raising savings directly via unspent business cash flow. Similar if lesser forces are at work in Benelux, Scandinavia and Switzerland. The combined personal and business savings add up to a private savings rate of 23% of GDP, and rising, for these countries together. This is far ahead of investment in business and housing – the difference creates a private-sector financial surplus. Though partly offset by government dis-saving of more than 1% of GDP in Germany, this surplus has no such outlet in Benelux, Scandinavia and Switzerland, which are mostly models of fiscal rectitude. So it expresses itself in a huge current surplus. As the rising euro in 2002–04 cut European export competitiveness, deficient demand also resulted, lowering incomes (and therefore savings as well).

The impact of north-central Europe's excess savings is softened outside Europe not only by deficits in Mediterranean Europe (including now France), but also in Britain and the former communist countries of eastern Europe. Thus the massive north-central current surplus of $250 billion in 2004 was reduced by $80 billion of net combined deficit in France (only slight in 2004, though larger in 2005), Spain, Italy, Portugal and Greece, and by a further $50 billion of UK current deficit. The resulting western European surplus was $120 billion. As this includes the dampening effect of weak domestic demand on income and savings, it can be considered the structural contribution of Europe to the global structural surplus. Some of it was absorbed by eastern European countries' deficits, but nearly $100 billion has to be pooled into the global problem, which is mostly played out in Asian-US trade and capital flows. (This number would be much larger without the much criticised government deficits in countries such as Germany, France, Italy and Britain.)

During 2005, the north-central European surpluses changed little – despite higher oil costs – but rapid demand growth in the Mediterranean countries and eastern Europe has sharply increased their deficits, virtually eliminating the European element in the global surplus glut. Instead a rapidly worsening imbalance within Europe itself has developed, with alarming implications for the durability of some Mediterranean countries' membership of the monetary union.

The 2004 current surpluses of the countries considered here – using the western European surplus of $120 billion as its contribution to the problem – totalled $500 billion (see Figure 1). Although this does not account for the full US current deficit of $670 billion that year (close to $800 billion in 2005), adding in the OPEC surplus and taking account of the cyclical surpluses in Canada and Latin America more than takes care of the difference. In other words, about three-quarters of the US deficit was structural, 'using up' these structural surpluses. The other quarter was trivial on a world scale. The structural element in this surplus redistributed itself during 2005 – sharply up in China, down in Europe – while the US deficit grew larger for cyclical reasons (offset by larger oil exporters' surpluses). But although a strong US downswing could – indeed, on the forecasts here is likely to – cut oil exporters' surpluses, cutting the structural Asian surplus will require either a drastic global recession or major policy changes that may only be achievable through western pressure.

While the structural surpluses are the chief manifestations of financial imbalance, they are the tip of the iceberg: below the surface lies the scale of savings relative to the capital needs of the economy. The savings data are the bedrock of this analysis, and the justification for Mr Bernanke's talk of an 'Asian savings glut'. US national savings were less than 14% of GDP in 2004, at just over $1.6 trillion. They have in effect been 'crowded out' over several years by surpluses flowing in from abroad. The national savings of China alone were more than half this in dollar terms, on a GDP only one-seventh of that of the United States. China's national savings rate was a staggering half of GDP in 2004.

Figure 5 **Gross national savings**
2004

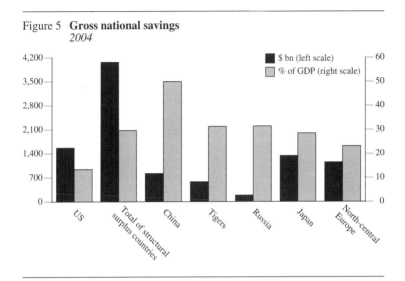

China and the Asian Tigers had savings of $1.45 trillion, Japan
had $1.33 trillion of private-sector savings, and the north-central
European countries' private savings were $1.14 trillion. Even
Russia's savings were $180 billion. The total of these savings
was over $4 trillion, two and a half times US savings. The ratio
of this $4 trillion to their combined GDP of $13.7 trillion (less
than 20% above the United States) was 30%, more than twice
America's 14%. This excessive desire for surpluses and savings
is the root cause of global financial imbalances.

2

Excess savings:
alternative effects and responses

An excessive propensity to save in a group of countries, as described here, can lead to only a limited variety of effects or responses:

1 **Higher private investment.** For investment to be higher than it would be otherwise, and use up the excess saving, the required rate of return on new assets has to be driven down. Such a lower rate of return would be a natural thing to expect if the supply of funds (saving) is boosted. In pre-Keynesian, classical economics, this is the normal, orthodox response.

2 **Lower private savings.** Without any changes in public policy, a lower rate of return might also (on reasonable though not invariably correct assumptions) be expected to lessen the attraction of private saving, whether in the glut countries or (more likely) elsewhere. Again this is a natural classical response.

3 **Easier monetary policy.** Easier money in non-glut countries

could use up excess savings in a number of ways. First, by validating and promoting a lower rate of interest (the fundamental cost of capital) it could induce a combination of higher investment and lower savings, provoking via policy the two responses already described. Second, where an economy is below full employment (whether or not caused by the savings glut) it could induce growth in domestic demand and net imports.

4 Easier fiscal policy. The government can directly dis-save or invest, offsetting the savings glut, by shifting towards deficit financing. (This was Keynes's last-resort remedy in the Depression, and Keynesians' first-resort remedy for any slowdown since 1945.)

5 Depression of demand, income and output. If none of the above occurs on sufficient scale, the potential savings glut will express itself as deficient demand, lowering output and incomes to the level where the saving out of such income is no longer higher than investment. The investment in such scenarios generally includes a large measure of unwanted inventory, as sales fall short of businesses' expectations. This inventory hangover lowers future demand – i.e. raises further the potential savings surplus. Demand, income and output enter a downward spiral.

The story here is of how various combinations of the first four responses, in various countries, have enabled the fifth, Depression, to be avoided – and of how a major risk of Depression, or liquidity trap, still exists. The story has already been suggested in the analysis of the meaning of 'excessive saving' (the propensity to save, so-called ex-ante saving): i.e. the savings people and businesses desire to save ahead of the event, rather than what they are actually able to save in the event. This ex-ante savings rate cannot be directly measured, as saving is only known after the event, ex post. As measured after the event, saving always equals investment (investment is demand or output, less consumption; saving is income less consumption). The saving that people originally wished to do can only be the subject of conjecture. It is through the presence of any of the first four responses listed above that the excess in originally intended saving can be inferred.

The US economy, which has been the central 'user' of excessive Asian savings, initiated responses 1–4 above in that order. First, there was higher investment in the bubble, with a wealth effect that induced lower personal savings. When the bubble burst, the Fed slashed interest rates, reinforcing the fall in personal savings by inducing huge increases in borrowing (more important than lower contractual savings in such vehicles as pension funds and mortgage repayments). The large 2001 tax cut (3) came close behind. When the stockmarket and the economy continued to languish during 2002, the approach was more of the same: another large tax and interest rate cut in 2003 to reinforce the 'Baghdad bounce'. The result has been two years of boom. Policy prescriptions were far more confused in 2001–04 in the euro zone, with correspondingly feeble results until recently.

Why 'invest more' did not work: the bubble, 1998–2000

The story starts with the Asian Crisis of 1997–98. 'Irrational exuberance' was Alan Greenspan's verdict on the US stockmarket before it all started, in December 1996. The Dow Jones Index was at 6,400 and the more representative S&P index at 740. At the peak of the bubble, three and a half years later in spring–summer 2000, the Dow reached a peak 75% higher at 11,300, and the S&P had more than doubled to 1,520. The Nasdaq 100 index – the epicentre of tech-bubble folly – had gone up 5.5 times over the same period, from 840 to 4,700. How did Mr Greenspan react to this huge increase in irrationality and exuberance? He encouraged it. Why? At least partly as an indirect response to the 1997 Asian crisis and its aftermath, the massive flow of Asian funds (and repatriated US speculative capital) to the 'safe haven' of the United States. The heavy flow of European capital to the United States began at about the same time, but the state of Europe was not a policy concern to the US authorities.

Increases in interest rates to quell irrational exuberance were put on hold in 1997, partly to avoid reinforcing the already devastating financial consequences of the Asian crisis. In late 1998, in mid-boom for America and Europe, the grossly heightened speculative fever arising from excessive cheap funding (conspicuously in Japanese yen, where a severe recession was coinciding with the Asian crisis) led to the spectacular bankruptcy of Long-Term Capital Management – Russian financial collapse and default being merely its contingent cause. US interest rates were cut three times by Mr Greenspan in seriously misconceived or at best exag-

Figure 6 **Pre-tax profit**
% of shareholders' equity, US non-financial companies

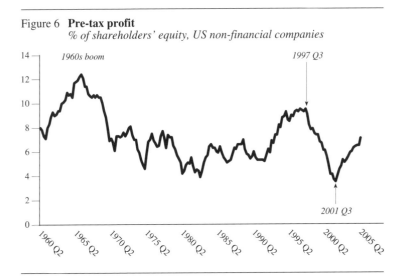

gerated anxiety over liquidity. This fuelled the last stage of the stockmarket's stratospheric rise.

The increase in underlying profitability in US business was the true source of the strong 1990s stockmarket. But it was largely over by the middle of the decade: non-financial companies' pre-tax return on net equity nearly doubled from 5.5% in 1990–91 to over 9% by the last quarter of 1994. The stockmarket boom had little to do with high technology, which was just as powerful an innovative factor in the 1980s, when profitability changed little, and the mid-to-late 1990s, when it fell. The drive after 1990 for 'shareholder value' was the root cause of improved profitability, arising (as in Japan after 1997) from 'restructuring'. The search for shareholder value was reinforced by the high cost of borrowing after the turnaround to lower inflation caused by

33

the stringent monetary policy of Paul Volcker, Mr Greenspan's predecessor as chairman of the Fed from 1979 to 1987. Hostile takeovers may not have generated much improvement in overall shareholder value in many instances, as mergers and acquisitions are notoriously unproductive in many, even most cases. But the fear of predators certainly changed behaviour in the managements wishing to survive. (This is the 'Admiral Byng' effect: after the British admiral was shot on a ship's quarterdeck for losing Minorca in 1756, Voltaire remarked that the English 'put an admiral to death now and then, to encourage the others'.)

Once the US corporate return on equity reached 9%, the natural reaction of businesses was 'more of that please'. They wanted more assets on which to earn such returns. Capital spending had been leading the 1990s economic advance since mid-1992, soon after the start of the upswing of profitability; by 1997 the growth rate of real business capital expenditure had been over 10% a year for five years. As Kingsley Amis, a British novelist, once (in a different context) remarked: 'More means worse.' Economists use the euphemism 'diminishing returns', and it is no coincidence that pre-tax returns to equity, having been on a 9%-plus plateau from late 1994 to 1997, relapsed – just as the capital expenditure growth rate achieved double figures, and stayed there for two and a half years until the bubble burst in mid-2000.

Profitability did not just shrink autonomously, however. The Asian savings excess dates from the Asian crisis, starting in the fourth quarter of 1997 – the same quarter in which the profit downswing began. Asia's economic and financial collapse, with massive devaluations, spurred a frantic search for exports. It was the start of the great surge into surplus. Pricing power weakened in western manufacturing, hitting profits. The concomitant flow of capital to the West underpinned not only booming stock prices, but also the easy debt financing of capital expenditure that helped erode profitability further, through excess capacity. An aspect of the process was upward pressure on the dollar in the late 1990s because of Asian (and European) flows. By putting downward pressure on US manufacturing profits, the high dollar played a part in the substitution of capital inflows for US domestic savings. Industrial capacity utilisation actually fell during the late 1990s, uniquely for a boom period. Just as the stockmarket and economy entered the full flower of leveraged boom, their foundations were being eroded. (The Y2K scare over millennial computer break-downs, a significant influence on Mr Greenspan, added to the spending excess.) The 2–3 year bust starting in mid-2000 was the first example of deflation resulting from balance sheets being trashed by excessive savings inflows from Asia. In this case, Asian surplus flows clearly were not the only factor behind the bubble and bust. But, starting at a crucial phase of the upswing, they reinforced and prolonged it. In an interactive process, excess saving led to lower returns and higher investment via a financial bubble.[3]

The fallacy of 'invest more for the future'

Incidentally, this experience argues against one plausible response to such savings flows: that the West should use the funds to 'invest more' – to 'store up' the benefit of the inflows for the future, for example to take care of future pension funding needs as populations age. It is a fallacy because increasing capital investment in such a fashion depresses returns and profitability; otherwise the savings could not be considered excessive. It can therefore only happen in the private sector in a context in which normal return expectations are distorted by a financial bubble, giving the illusion of strong returns where they are actually falling. Thus, during 1998–2000, financial returns to shareholders looked good, as share prices rose. Yet the return on capital in companies was falling, as excessive investment and the build-up of debt and interest depressed profit margins. It was essentially a liquidity-driven boom, with European and Asian surpluses providing much of the liquidity, reinforced by the Fed. Once share prices had risen to the point where they were liable to 'fall under their own weight', interest rates just happened to have risen enough to constrict liquidity. 'It never rains, but it pours' – and the bubble burst.

The heavy investment in 1998–2000 depended on company managements responding to misconceived shareholder expectations – and in the process undermining them ('more means worse'). It really is not possible for the economy to 'store up future value' with investments that initially yield a poor return. If people knew enough about what the future will require, they would pay for the value with adequate returns right away. In reality, people, including company managements, know very little about precise future needs. The fallacy of knowing the future lies behind much misguided criticism of investor 'short-termism'. If money were spent on the priorities of most 'long-termists', the bankruptcy court would not be far away.

Even where forecasts are right about future needs, the fallacy persists. Suppose you overinvest in correctly chosen productive assets now, to use up excess savings and provide for a future time when population ageing reduces the flow of saving and increasing consumption needs. The overinvestment will create excess capacity, driving down prices. Existing productive assets will be rendered unprofitable, and probably the new assets too. The result is just like a regular bubble: investment stops as it becomes unprofitable, and the economy goes into recession, cutting investment further. Either way, 'investing for the future', a natural financial strategy for individuals, does not work as a real capital spending strategy for society, where the investment is physical, in productive assets, rather than putting money aside.

Only if economies (or societies) lower their expectations of reasonable investment returns can the 'invest more' policy work. But this creates two problems:

- Requiring strong returns is a crucial condition of healthy economic development and should not be abandoned because of the peculiarities of Asian savings behaviour.
- The foreign savings inflows tend to drive up asset prices, at least initially, raising expectations of easy capital gains – the reverse of the lower expectations that are more appropriate.

It is partly because we are still not at the end of this 'bubble' phase of the Asian surplus effects that economies keep going.

The only plausible source for an 'invest more' policy is government investment, especially on infrastructure. This sort of policy, advocated by Keynes in the depression of the 1930s, was adopted by Japan in the 1990s after its late-1980s bubble. Japan's legendary waste and corruption in public projects illustrate the severe limits on such an 'invest more' approach, which is largely self-defeating. Once capital ceases to be perceived as scarce and costly, and starts being thrown around indiscriminately, the hoped-for returns from investment melt away. (See page 124.)

Lower private savings: inflation of asset prices – the bubble wealth effect

Private savings rates do not necessarily go down because of lower interest rates. Lower real interest rates (the rate of interest less the rate of inflation) are the true cost of capital, and are driven down by the savings glut. By themselves such lower real rates do not necessarily lower western savings. It is the interaction with prices of real assets – mostly homes and equities – that is crucial to personal savings behaviour.

Before looking at the complexity of personal behaviour, consider the relatively simple case of business savings, which are depreciation plus retained profits (after interest, tax and dividends). Here, the chief driver is profitability itself. In the bubble, business profitability and the spending side of the capital account – investment – were intimately related to one another. After the bubble burst, businesses in both America and Europe reacted to create surpluses: first they cut capital spending, leaving cash flow with which to repay debt; then they raised their cash flow by cutting labour costs. In Japan this had been true since 1997.

If the bubble is accepted as the first phase of the reaction to excessive Asian savings, business behaviour since 2001 can be regarded as exacerbating the surpluses to be absorbed. For Japan and north-central Europe this has already been described. Suffice it to say that in the rest of Europe, and especially the United States, upward shifts in business profitability, and downward pressures on capital spending, have added to the global surplus/ savings glut since the bubble burst. Business savings have gone up, in other words, as real interest rates have gone down. This is another example of the importance of getting cause and effect the right way round. It was not that lower interest rates from 2001 would cause lower business saving: it was higher post-bubble business saving that was a major cause of lower interest rates. Reversing the direction of causation reverses the association of savings and real interest rates, as is generally true of cause and effect in economics.

Personal savings can involve a paradox. In an economy with little or no personal holdings of real assets other than owner-occupied homes, low real interest rates might require households to raise savings. Suppose people wish to have a pension pot on reaching 65. If real interest rates are low, the savings rate will need to be higher to accumulate the pot. And low real returns will mean low annuity rates after the age of 65, the pension pay-out period, so that a larger pot will anyhow be required for a desired rate of pension (relative to previous earned income). Thus lower real rates force both a higher proportionate savings rate for a given pot, and a larger pot for a given ratio of pension to previous income. Both these forces generally result in higher savings. Conversely, higher real rates will permit a given ratio of eventual pension to current salary at a lower rate of saving. This idea is uncomfortable for classical economics, as it means that offering a lower rate of return tends to increase savings, and vice versa.

If we introduce personal holdings of equities, a build-up of Asian surpluses flowing into America and the bubble, some things become clearer and others less so. How does the rate of return get lowered by the inflow of surpluses? Why, by rising asset prices: the bubble. For those with assets, the achievement of a desired pension pot is advanced at a stroke by the stockmarket boom. So although the rate of return has been lowered, the all-in return to asset-holders has received a boost. This higher all-in rate of return acts like the higher real rates of the preceding paragraph: by making the pot more easily achieved, it lowers the need to save. This is the wealth effect, leading to a lower savings rate.

This deals with only half the problem, however. The lower real returns resulting from soaring asset prices mean that the annuity/pension payable from a given pot will be less (especially given increasing longevity). This implies a rising pot – evidence for this being widely publicised and large shortfalls in US and UK company pension plans on proper calculations. It is hard to resist the conclusion that 'Anglo-Saxon' households are adopting an 'ostrich' strategy on this. It looks like a case of inverted Alzheimer's disease. In real Alzheimer's, old people forget the past. With inverted Alzheimer's, middle-aged people forget the future.

Savings needed at 2% and 4% constant real interest rates
Working life assumptions (with the same real interest rates used for both working life accumulation of the pension pot, and the resulting annuity paid out from the pot after retirement)

45	year working life (20–65)
20	year retirement (65–85)
3%	annual growth of real income during working life
60%	target pension as % of final salary (fixed for life)
£50,000	final salary

With 2% real interest rates, the required pot is £1,009,456 and the share of salary over the working life required to achieve it is 28.1% (with this share held constant throughout the assumed 45 years of working life).

With 4% real interest rates, the required pot falls by two-thirds to £342,289 and the share of salary is dramatically reduced, to 5.7%.

The strong variation of these figures in relation to what appear to be small changes in real interest rates illustrates the difficulties in the pension debate and for company pension fund provision. Was it Einstein who described compound interest as one of the strongest forces in nature? In reality, pension plans invest heavily (particularly when the members are early in their careers) in higher-risk, higher-return equities, where the long-term real rate of return has been 7%, well above the 2% and 4% considered here. But for this, the pension problems facing most company plans would have been radically worse.

The worst form of inverted Alzheimer's is that the Asian (and European) surpluses are likely on current trends to cause havoc with personal finances through excessive household debt and borrowing. This is the true source of lower savings from lower interest rates. Household savings in aggregate are the net result of saving by savers and net borrowing by households in excess of new home building. With nearly 300 million people in America, for example, there are plenty of households contributing to pension plans and simultaneously paying down mortgages; there are also plenty of households borrowing to buy houses, pay for children's education and so on, so that their consumer spending exceeds their income. If a house-price boom based on capital inflows and fuelled by borrowing drives up consumer spending, the savings rate will be lower, and reasonably closely connected to the low rate of interest. But, of course, the natural ambition – a house with no mortgage and an adequate pension pot at age 65 – is being put on hold by the borrowing. Household debt has to be repaid out of earned income during a working lifetime. Building up debt on the back of higher house prices beyond a certain point is inverted Alzheimer's in this sense: it is in denial of this future requirement. It is this debt behaviour that is the 'bubble' element in western responses to the Asian savings glut in recent years.

But complacency arising from the belief that capital gains will provide the pension pot needed to meet expectations also suggests a major problem arising from lower rates of return on the assets side of personal balance sheets. This mostly concerns America and Britain, where employer-sponsored pensions are important; continental Europeans have much greater reliance on tax-financed public provision with an overlay of private wealth. The resulting equity culture means the wealth effect on saving has been far greater in America and Britain. The continental Europeans have their own peculiar exposure to a huge rise in taxation to fund extravagant public pension promises. But the British and Americans, via public insurance vehicles to make up for private pension scheme failures, may also find themselves with unexpectedly large tax increases on account of widespread failures in private provisions.

Post-bubble monetary and fiscal ease: US policy

US monetary policy was aggressively easy for three and a half years, from early 2001 to mid-2004. Although the bubble peaked in the spring of 2000 – as seen in retrospect, and after numerous revisions of the GDP data for the last three quarters of 2000 – the stockmarket was strong until the end of August. The August average for the S&P index, the representative Wall Street measure, was actually the peak monthly average of the bull market, ahead of springtime monthly averages. In October and as late as December that year well-known US economists were still predicting a soft rather than hard landing for the US economy. (Hard landing is code for virtually no growth, but without necessarily the two quarters of negative GDP that is the technical definition of a recession.) It now turns out that the hard landing was already well under way, for the economy as well as the stockmarket. GDP had fallen as early as the third quarter, recovering a little in the fourth; it was relapsing from just under 5% growth in the year to the second quarter of 2000. Growth was negative again in the first and third quarters of 2001, so that by the second half of 2001 growth from the year before was only just above zero. As sustainable trend growth is (and was) 3% or a little more, the shortfall from this neutral rate was a large three percentage points.

The initial sharp cuts in short-term interest rates were a simple, conventional reaction to the hard landing. The speed and size of the cuts needed was increased by the mistakes made during the bubble. Alan Greenspan carried on talking up the bubble until October 1999, only half a year before it burst – in clear and unjustified contrast to his three years earlier talk of 'irrational exuberance'. Anti-inflationary interest rate hikes to keep the economy under control in late 1999 and early 2000 were a classic case of 'too much, too late'. Instead of damping the boom, the Fed aggravated the violence of the cycle and, because Asian inflows had been doing the same, the downswing was correspondingly fierce.

One difference between a bubble and a boom is that after a bubble the distortions introduced in the upswing are so great that it can take two recessions to remove them. (Each boom has its own particular set of distortions that become its Achilles heel. Usually, they involve overextension of the original driving factor that created the boom to start with – in this case business investment.) After the 1999–2000 bubble, it was not so much two recessions as a hard landing and an extremely weak recovery, despite strong policy stimulation (monetary and fiscal). But one implication of the argument in this book is that monetary and fiscal ease have been used to avoid working out the distortions, and that these will soon come back to hit us with another downswing.

Recoveries from recession in the United States, where cycles have generally been quite violent, are usually very rapid. But this one was not. After five quarters to the third quarter of 2001 with an average growth rate of just over zero (and three of the five quarters down from the one before), the economy grew at only a feeble 1.75% in the subsequent six quarters. This rate was still well below the 3%-plus trend or potential rate. So from the end of the hard landing as such (in the third quarter of 2001) the shortfall of GDP from its potential level widened substantially further, an extremely unusual and malign development. By early 2003 the economy had been through just under three years at an average growth rate of 1%. By May 2003, fearing deflation, the Fed had cut short-term interest rates to 1%, which was unprecedentedly low and significantly below the inflation rate.

In America and Europe, the end of the bubble resulted in the business sector adding to the potential depression of demand arising from Eurasian surpluses. As the bubble was led by capital expenditure, then burst because of the resulting erosion of profit margins, the reaction in the downswing – and the reason the hard landing started to turn into a deflationary spiral – was to cut capital spending and then raise profitability by cutting jobs and other costs. It is easy to see the deflationary implications of this. But it is useful to view it in terms of flows of funds: each sector's saving minus its investment. In the United States, by spring 2000, business's capital spending exceeded its saving (depreciation plus retained profits) by 2–3% of GDP. By 2003 this had switched to saving (boosted by cost cuts) exceeding capital expenditure by 3–4% of GDP: i.e. this switch shifted the business balance by six percentage points of GDP. The resulting business surplus can be added to the Asian surplus that was financing the capital inflow. With the latter at 5–6% of GDP, the two combined were 9% of GDP. This is a measure of the deficit that had to be run by the combined household and government sectors to keep the economy on an even keel. It is no surprise that such a huge scale of policy stimulation was needed. There has never been anything approaching it in a serious economy in peacetime.

While monetary policy became dramatically easy, arguably the 'heavy lifting' in stimulative policy was done by large tax cuts, an even more extravagant fiscal easing than the monetary stimulus. In January 2001, President George W. Bush came to power committed to tax cuts anyhow. The timing was fortuitous. A large tax cut was proposed and easily passed by Congress in spring 2001. As a result, between 2000 and 2002 the US public-sector balance shifted into deficit by 5.5% of GDP, from more than 1.5% surplus in 2000 to 3.75% deficit in 2002. Of this 5.5% shift, some 4.5% was attributable to policy changes – mostly the tax cut – and the remaining 1% to cyclical losses of tax revenue arising from the recession.

By early 2003, the economy was still languishing with growth below trend. The Iraq war was looming, sapping confidence. With newly elected majorities in both houses of Congress, President Bush implemented another large tax cut, from July 2003. In the second half of 2003, the US public-sector deficit ran at over 5%

of GDP. Tax-cutting policy worsened the balance by 1% of GDP, but some of this was offset by stronger growth giving an autonomous cyclical boost to tax revenue. The combination of large fiscal deficits and the household boom based on easy money – by this time short-term rates had been cut to 1% – coming on top of the post-war 'Baghdad bounce', finally goosed the economy into a boom.

Vibrant economic activity revived tax revenue in 2004 (and 2005), so that the deficit narrowed slightly. Nonetheless, the 2004 US public-sector balance was 6% of GDP worse than in 2000, before the tax cuts. In addition, monetary stimulus had caused the personal sector deficit to enlarge by 2.5% of GDP. This combined shift of 8.5% of GDP offset the business-sector balance improvement by over 6% plus a 1.5% worsening of the current-account deficit, from 2000's already large 4.25% to 2004's 5.75%. So the business sector boom-bust partly induced by Eurasian surpluses, together with the increase in the surpluses themselves, was offset by a huge policy-induced boost to US household and government borrowing. Roughly two-thirds of the extra borrowing was being done by government, and one-third by households.

The euro zone's mixed policy response

In the euro zone, such a clear illustration of the shifting flows of funds cannot be made, as it is muddled up with the surplus in Germany and the rest of north-central Europe. The statistics are also vastly inferior. But one of the effects of the monetary union – probably its only major plus-point to date – has been the unification of capital markets, assisting businesses in achieving rapid capital-productivity gains: the same output is being gained from less capital, or more output from the same capital. European business has been throwing off capital. So the euro zone's business financial flows have been improving over the past few years for structural reasons, as well as the post-bubble cyclical restructuring outlined above, in a similar way to the United States.

On the household side, no general economic and monetary union (EMU) pattern can be shown. In Spain, a US/UK-style property boom has proceeded unchecked for years because eurozone interest rates have been low by Spanish standards. At the opposite end of the spectrum, Germany, growing and inflating the least of the EMU majors, and with the full force of excess savings on both demographic and now restructuring grounds, has seen personal savings grow as housing has declined. Between them come Italy, with German demographics but a poorer housing stock and Spanish reactions to euro interest rates; and France, with stronger demographics but closer to Germany in inflation. For both of these countries, household borrow-and-spend has been a gathering force.

Euro-zone fiscal policy was less fortuitously clear-cut than President Bush's. Apart from the responsibility being at the country level, not 'delegated' (or uplifted) to EMU, any co-ordination that existed was entirely and strongly concerned with eliminating all budget deficits. The background was the major cuts needed in France, Italy and Spain to bring their deficits below 3% of GDP and comply with the Maastricht criteria for EMU membership. Germany, the 'policeman' of EMU, understandably (and rightly) felt that such low deficits in the target year of 1997 might prove a flash in the pan without some continuing restraint of budgetary excesses. The EMU entrants were required to sign up in 1998 to the Stability and Growth Pact (SGP) by which 3% was to be the maximum – allowable only under duress, such as recession – with members committed to budget balance by 2005. This proposal was controversial (to say the least) even before the surplus problem emerged, with Germany in a conspicuous role. One paraphrase of the SGP, for example, was 'Stagnation and Grief Pact'. In the conditions actually prevailing after the bubble burst it was close to a disaster.

The tremendous boom in 1999–2000 actually took the weighted average euro-zone budget balance to a minuscule surplus in 2000 (0.1% of GDP). This was not all that impressive: massive bubble-based tax revenues took America and Britain to 1.5% surpluses in 2000 (excluding one-off UK mobile phone licence proceeds). Still, Italy and Spain got their deficits below 1% of GDP, giving them grounds for patting themselves on the back. However, the onset of recession in 2001 quickly took the gloss off this achievement. The worsening of euro-zone budgets in that year was just under 2% of GDP, only minimally less than the United States with its huge tax cut. At this point policy in the euro zone diverged sharply. Germany, father of the SGP, despite a major private-sector financial surplus that makes it part of the global surplus/deflation problem, decided to add fiscal policy deflation to its (and the world's) woes. Smaller countries (Belgium, Finland, Austria, Ireland and, before strong inflation took its toll, the Netherlands) and Spain emerged comparatively unscathed from the 2001 downswing and sided with Germany. France and Italy took the Anglo-American route and decided not just to accept budget deficits from cyclical tax revenue losses, but to add structural fiscal stimulus on top.

If full employment with low inflation is accepted as the goal of demand management, the euro zone failed utterly (hence the electoral rejection of existing governments in major continental countries recently). But this is not the only criterion for policy, so these fiscal policy responses must be seen in a broader context, bearing in mind that neither exchange rate nor interest rate determination is now within the power of national governments. With true political power still firmly in the hands of national governments – and subject to electorates (up to a point) – the confused and transitional nature of the current EMU/government balance of power is inevitable. In a (useful) sense, the severe test it is now being put to will determine more effectively than shallow political decisions in 1996–98 who can genuinely sustain the political integration that is the necessary and painful accompaniment of a true monetary union.

Germany has always been the most ardent advocate of political and economic union as a necessary (ideally pre-) condition of EMU. Suffering an excessive exchange rate on adopting the euro and the highest real interest rates (and bond yields) in the euro zone, as well as the demographic and restructuring deflation, it might be thought perverse to the point of masochism for Germany to have added fiscal tightness as a fifth source of demand restraint. But at least at the level of the ruling elite it had two other priorities: first, to make the monetary union, in which its ruling class has always been the most fervent and serious believer, a success; and second, to shed the excessive labour costs built up in 1990–97 as a result of German reunification. Quintuple German deflation (exchange-rate, monetary, fiscal, demographic and restructuring) may have caused three recessions in three years, but it has imposed labour-market flexibility – by brute force. As a result, Germany is now able to gain market share both within the euro zone and outside it, and probably over time to enjoy faster productivity growth, raising long-term income growth. Other countries' fiscal policies have reflected their own particular circumstances. These will be clearer after a look at how monetary policy was managed in the post-bubble stagnation.

The nature of the monetary union, still in its early days, ensured monetary policy was also confused, especially in appearance. Appearances and 'credibility' (market trust) are important for effective monetary policy: the US Fed's presentation of its policy has been assured, and its reputation is high, even if that policy can be quite severely criticised in its substance. Much public confusion about the policies of the European Central Bank (ECB) arises from the importance of Germany, which accounts for 30% of EMU GDP (the combination of deflationary factors in Germany, many related to the euro, is described above). But the ECB has to consider the whole of the euro zone, 70% of which is not Germany. With German inflation mostly in the 1–2% range, and growth minimal, why not ease monetary policy? The answer is because conditions are very different elsewhere. In Germany, the real three-month interbank interest rate has been

Figure 7 **ECB nominal repo rate**
'Real' cost adjusted for inflation in selected countries, %

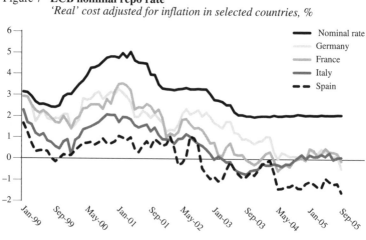

2% and falling since post-bubble 2001 and has become steadily less burdensome. But the real rate for France, Italy and especially Spain has been zero to negative for over two and a half years. For EMU as a whole, real short-term rates have been as low as in the United States. While its long-term trend growth has been weaker, the level of GDP vis-à-vis this trend has been less depressed than America's at the worst, and the inflation rate has stayed up stubbornly. This is why ECB policy could be regarded as in aggregate easier, or at least no tighter, than the Fed's.

The true source of slow euro-zone growth, apart from Germany's multiple deflation, is the dismal long-term trend (or 'potential') growth rate. This is caused by supply-side weaknesses such as excessive and distorted taxation, overregulation and, most conspicuously, labour-market rigidities that make it difficult and costly to fire people and place restrictions on working hours. These problems are not the subject here. Combined with now-static, EMU-wide, working-age-group growth, the effect of these productivity constraints on long-term growth trends is to cut it below 2% for the euro zone, more than 1% annually behind the US and 0.5% behind Britain. The effect of this feeble trend, alongside restrictive policies that have actually managed to get EMU GDP below it – if by less than the US at the worst of its hard landing (first quarter of 2003) – has been lethal to the global economic standing of the euro zone. Such is the price of the ill-considered rush to 'union'. But the positive result is that whatever (almost certainly reduced) monetary union emerges from current conditions will be a serious entity, unlike what was put together in 1991–99.

With monetary policy outside the control of euro-zone countries, it is only against this backdrop that we can see their fiscal policies in a proper perspective. France, which was close to average in terms of inflation rate and therefore real interest rates, pursued moderate budget stimulation after 2001, with no serious regard for the SGP. This has been largely successful: France's demand management policies have been closest to those of America and Britain. Its house-price boom has been strong. The economy has deviated relatively little from long-term trend growth rates. Its high unemployment, like its slow trend growth, are functions of labour-market and other supply-side policies, which include making it illegal to work hard – the 35-hour week – and are utterly unlike America's and Britain's. But from the standpoint of accommodating Eurasian surpluses, French policy has been increasingly successful.

The same is not true of Spain and Italy, which are also very different from one another. In Spain, the starting point was productivity at some 85% of the level in Germany, France and Italy (all of which were very close in real output per worker-hour in 1999); but having much lower labour costs, only about half Germany's. The natural effect of the fixed exchange rate regime was to ensure both faster growth than the rest of EMU – real income catch-up – and faster inflation, thereby achieving cost convergence. (Low inflation and currency appreciation was the alternative route chosen by Japan and Germany in the 1970s and 1980s.)

Faster Spanish inflation meant that the common interest rates and bond yields for the euro were much lower in real terms than for Germany and France. Though Spain's growth has not been impressive given its potential – and productivity trends have worsened – it is not for lack of demand. The house-price and real estate boom has equalled or surpassed that of America, Britain and France, fuelled by ultra-cheap money and price levels that were low to start with. Fiscal policy has been quite rightly concerned with stemming some of these speculative excesses, and the structural budget balance has tightened. Spain is thus able to look down on fellow euro-zone countries, neither breaching the SGP with budgetary ease, as France and Italy have done, nor resorting, as Germany has, to simple, recession-induced tax shortfalls. It is a feel-good mix to match America's in response to the inflow of the Asian savings glut.

Italy's policy has been seemingly like France's, but with key flaws. While its labour costs have grown only 0.5% a year faster than France's, its productivity growth has been negligible for the full seven years' existence of the euro. This is euro-sclerosis at its most extreme. A widening budget deficit has been needed as much to compensate with artificial stimulus for loss of export competitiveness vis-à-vis EMU 'partners' as to offset Eurasian surpluses. In the current global boom, with borrowing costs for Italians unprecedentedly low, mortgage finance growing at nearly 20% a year is adding to budget action to keep the economy on the move as Italy, the Cinderella of EMU, keeps seeing its market share poached by the ugly sisters to the north. But its unit labour costs have gone adrift by 15% compared with the rest of the euro zone since 1998, and the gap is widening by 2% a year (more compared with Germany, of course). Unlike Spain, Italy's labour costs when EMU started in 1999 were above Germany's, similar to France and Benelux. Eurasian surpluses are in effect papering over a crack that has become so wide that Italy will probably have to give up EMU membership (painfully) in a few years. The ready availability of Eurasian surpluses while problems are quietly swept under the carpet may do neither Italy nor its euro-zone partners any favours.

Britain's fortunate policy framework

In Britain, where the growth trend has not deteriorated, the shift of responsibility for setting interest rates from the government to the Bank of England (BoE) in May 1997 has been fortuitously helpful to handling the Asian savings excess, aside from its intrinsic merits. The government simply sets the BoE an inflation target and leaves it to set interest rates to achieve that target. This separation of the goal (or end) of monetary policy – constant inflation at 2% (now, for the consumer price index; 2.5% initially in 1997 for a modified version of the retail price index) – from the means (interest rates) has been highly beneficial in ways that go well beyond the simple removal of political temptations to meddle with rates. The single-tasked BoE has to be forward-looking, in a way the US Fed certainly is not. Setting rates with respect to a forecast of inflation two years hence (or whatever period is suitable) forces discipline on both the forecasting process and the discussion of appropriate rates. This can otherwise be only too easily influenced by short-term fluctuations in economic and financial market conditions and/or confidence, as has been normal in America.

Moreover, by imposing the inflation target as the framework for monetary policy, the BoE's independence removes the need and temptation for central bankers to involve and compromise themselves politically. It is common to hear central bankers express views on such matters as the budget deficit, rigidities in the labour market and so forth (all of them the subject of speeches by Fed and ECB members in recent years). Now the BoE simply has to say, for example about an increase in the government deficit, that achievement of the inflation target will require higher interest rates the larger the government deficit is. Whether the central bankers approve or disapprove of the fiscal policy – which is politically irrelevant and arguably unconstitutional – becomes irrelevant to their monetary role. Note the contrast with the ECB, which not only sets its own targets – in this case for broad money growth as well as inflation – but also is independent by international treaty (Maastricht) rather than by (revocable) legislative action. The ECB has significantly raised perceptions that its policy is unduly tight by combining interest rate decisions with scolding various member states for policy errors, which in a democracy is not within its remit. Mr Greenspan has been only marginally less gratuitous.

The BoE remit was well suited to handling the Asian savings glut and the bubble and bust of 1999–2002. The BoE was lucky in that at the start of the new regime in mid-1997, inflation was about on the set target, growth was about on trend, and so was the level of GDP. The remit came down to keeping growth on trend (2.5% on most independent estimates) and to avoiding any build-up of inflationary pressures from overheating or disinflationary pressures from inadequate demand. As above-trend growth pressure mounted in the bubble, inflation forecasts tended to rise, so it was felt that interest rates were increased in plenty of time. But this timely shift of monetary policy toward higher interest rates, combined with the Asian surplus sloshing about looking for a well-run safe haven, meant that sterling rose. In Britain's very open economy, this created immediate downward pressure on prices – the target of monetary policy – as well as on export demand and manufacturing profitability. As a result, easing of demand pressure reinforced cheaper imports to cut inflation.

While freedom of the flow of capital into and out of Britain has never been threatened, such flows have also (fortuitously) been less problematic than for the United States in recent years.

Britain has an 'unencumbered' currency. The US dollar, however, has reserve currency status. It is an uncomfortable position, as funds move into and out of the dollar for reasons unconnected to the US economy, but it is also profitable. The US financial industry benefits hugely from such flows. But this position has been massively complicated in recent years by China's pegging its currency to the dollar, together with its emergence as a major trading power. Britain has been able to get the best of both worlds on this point: it is a major beneficiary of global financial flows, but without compromise to its monetary independence.

3

International monetary consequences: the New Dollar Area

China pegged the yuan to the dollar in 1994 in good faith as a stabilising measure after the major 1994 devaluation. This followed loss of monetary control and 30% inflation in 1993. Ironically, the yuan–dollar peg has been a major destabilising force in recent years. In effect, it prevented the adjustment of exchange rates that would otherwise have occurred from early 2002. The dollar, unlike sterling, cannot float freely if other countries insist on pegging their currencies to it, in its role as the world's reserve currency. After private capital flows into the dollar dried up in early 2002, it should have been possible for it to depreciate to the level at which investors recovered their appetite, probably with higher bond yields as part of the bargain. This might or might not have involved improvement in the US current deficit, or perhaps the lessening of some of the Eurasian surpluses. But it would have balanced out the financing of such imbalances with the cost-benefit analysis of investors providing the counterpart capital flows. The drastic cuts in US short-term

Figure 8 **Weighted average exchange rates adjusted for relative unit labour costs**
Except China based on relative consumer prices, April 2001 = 100

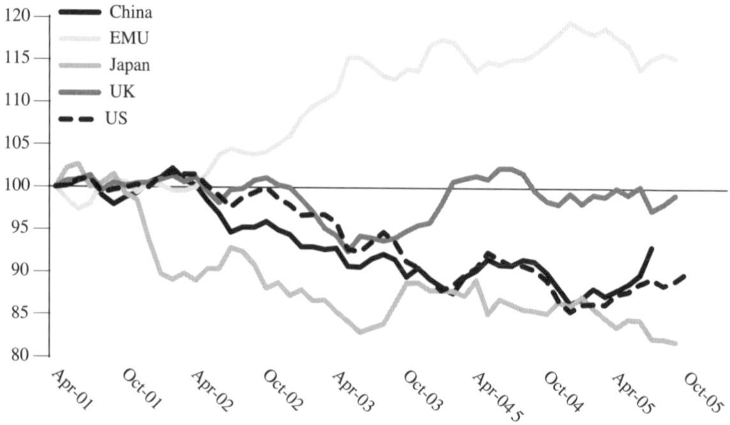

Sources: IMF; Federal Reserve broad index (US)

interest rates in 2001–03 were at least partly intended to achieve this prophylactic decline in the dollar. Because of the yuan–dollar peg, it did not happen.

Between the yuan–dollar peg's establishment in 1994 and now, China has made a quantum leap in global economic significance. It is the dominant economy regionally, given its greater participation in foreign trade than Japan. The yuan–dollar peg gave support to the Pacific region during the gross upheavals of the 1997–98 Asian crisis. But the increased size of China, and its huge advantage in cost competitiveness, has been an increasing concern for Asian countries from Japan downwards. Over the past 15–20 years they have been 'hollowed out' by China's takeover of much of the world's manufacturing. The combination of the yuan–dollar peg and the dollar's decline from early 2002 confronted Asian competitors with the risk of even greater Chinese cost competitiveness. Their response was what we call the New Dollar Area (NDA), a semi-fixed-rate currency zone including China, Japan and the Asian Tigers, bound together by the mortar of fear – fear of China. Japan and those Asian Tigers without existing dollar pegs managed their exchange rates by intervention to ensure they stayed competitive – not with the dollar, as US competition is not a problem, but with China and its yuan.

As a result, the 12–15% cut in America's real exchange rate over three years from early 2002 – i.e. the gain in its global cost competitiveness with trading partners – was roughly matched by the real trade-weighted yuan exchange rate and China's cost advantage – and, surprise, surprise, by Japan's, together with that of much of the rest of the Asian Tigers. In effect, the dollar was able to devalue only against the euro and sterling. Almost all the Eurasian structural surpluses corresponding to the US deficit lie in Pacific Asia (Japan, China and the Tigers), with which America made no gain in cost competitiveness. Those countries had their costs heavily trimmed vis-à-vis Europe's, and the European market share gains that resulted were achieved much more by Asian rather than American exporters. And in the US market itself, Asians were able to gain share from Europeans faster than had been occurring in any case. With Asian/US competitiveness locked in place by the NDA structure, America's US expansion raised its imports and ensured no deficit reduction was achieved by the dollar devaluation. On the contrary, between 2000 and

Figure 9 **Trade growth**
China and world, %

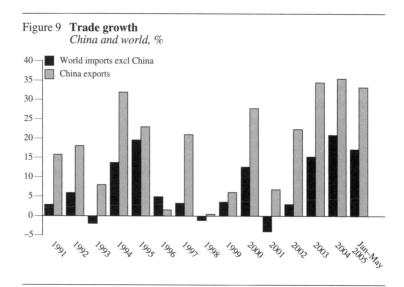

2005 the US current-account deficit rose from 4% of GDP to 6–6.5%. Some adjustment!

That China had no need of extra cost competitive advantage can be seen by examining its export growth vis-à-vis world trade (see Figure 9). In 2002, as the recovery from the bubble started, world imports excluding China grew by 3%; China's exports grew a strong 22%. Yet pre-yuan depreciation relative costs at the end of 2001 will have underlain this performance. China certainly did not need an extra 12% of cost competitiveness. It hung on to the dollar partly through inertia and partly through an understandable desire for stability, given the upheavals of 1993–94 and its relative strength in (and immunity from) the Asian crisis of 1997–98, in which the rigidity of the dollar peg was a help.

But increasingly China's policy looks like crude, muscle-bound mercantilism: a simple, zero-sum-game attempt to grab export market share by exchange rate manipulation. Though the rest of the Asian NDA countries tag along behind willingly enough, Chinese policymakers must take a major share of responsibility for the more extreme destabilising effects of Asian surpluses which are the subject of this book. But before looking at the global consequences, the effects of China's policy on its own development, and on its savings and surplus, must be understood. It is a classic case of how mercantilism tends over time to damage the apparent market share winner, via a variety of feedbacks.

In 2002–04, China's depreciation seemed superficially innocuous, because its current-account surplus (unlike that of Japan and the Asian Tigers) barely increased. It was possible to claim that the yuan–dollar peg was not causing Chinese under-valuation. But the underlying dynamics were not simply a matter of short-term shifts in the trade balance, and the gross under-valuation is now being revealed by the exploding surplus that emerged in 2005. The key is the domestic Chinese boom induced by the downswing of the yuan. To hold its rate against the dollar, China and other Asian NDA countries managing their exchange rates had to intervene heavily to buy dollars and sell their own currencies. This led to vast flows of liquidity being flushed out into their domestic financial systems as well as huge accumu-lations of dollar reserves, with important consequences in 2005 (see page 104).

Soaring domestic liquidity created a credit-financed invest-ment boom in China; in Japan it underpinned the end of the long spiral of deflation (see page 88). China's boom sucked in a huge flow of imports, keeping its Chinese surplus down. Most of these imports, apart from energy and raw materials, were from Japan and the Tigers. If we regard the Asian end of the NDA – China, Japan and the Tigers (the entire Pacific rim) – as a semi-fixed-rate block, the undervaluation of their currencies as a group is demonstrated by their rapidly growing collective surplus: the distribution of that surplus was simply loaded away from China and into the others by the Chinese investment boom temporarily sucking in imports from Japan and the Tigers. As this Chinese domestic boom unwinds, the primary role of yuan undervaluation emerges.

China's official figures for real GDP growth cannot be believed. Growth for the past ten years is said to have varied between 7% and 10%, an incredibly narrow range given the importance of investment, which is invariably a more volatile part of demand than consumption – it is not far short of half GDP. The nominal data (i.e. the original numbers before adjustment for price changes) can be adjusted by separately published inflation figures to give a rough idea of real growth; this shows an altogether more plausible cyclicality. In 1998–99, affected by the Asian crisis, nominal growth was only 5% in each year. For six quarters running it averaged about 4%; allowing for slight deflation at the time, implied real growth was only 4–5%. By contrast, in 2004 nominal growth was 16.5%. Domestic inflation was about 3%, with much of the 4% consumer price index gain reflecting the higher costs of imported oil, food and raw materials, so real GDP growth was 13–14%. In other words, China's trend growth is about 8–9%, as claimed, but with a much more plausibly violent cyclical range of

Figure 10 **China: GDP and trade and domestic demand**
% change over 4 quarters

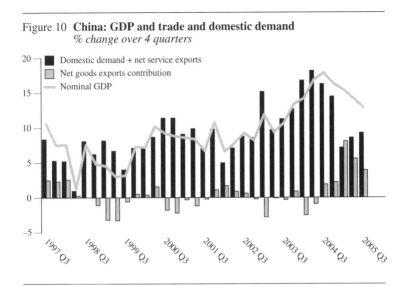

plus or minus 4–5% (i.e. from 4% to 13%) rather than the plus or minus 1.5% implicit in the published real growth figures.

The importance of this lies in the domestic boom it reveals in 2003–04, when nominal domestic demand was up by 16–18% on the year earlier level for three quarters at the peak. Net exports made a slightly negative contribution because the surge of imports was temporarily even greater than the surge of exports. As the domestic boom has inevitably ebbed away, the surge of exports has continued. Import growth has fallen back, in line with domestic demand – though imports of parts for assembly and export have continued to grow fast. Year-on-year domestic demand growth for the first three quarters of 2005 averaged about 8% nominally (perhaps 6% in real terms). Import growth fell from 38% in 2004 to 16% in 2005. Net exports have contributed

65

nearly half the growth of nominal GDP and more than that in real terms, given little if any inflation of export prices and continually rising costs of imported oil and raw materials. But for export growth, the fall-back of domestic demand would probably have led to an immediate hard landing in response to the excessive capital spending of 2003–04. Export growth has provided jobs and wages in export industries that have softened (so far) the drop in domestic demand growth. For a fuller description of this boom and likely bust, see the Appendix.

Several consequences of the yuan–dollar peg for the global economy worsened financial imbalances in 2003–04:

- Excessive export competitiveness in Asia, which much increased its surplus.
- Fear of deflation in 2002 and early 2003 as the United States was unable to raise demand by rebalancing overseas accounts with exports. This provoked extreme monetary and fiscal measures in spring 2003 that sowed the seeds of a debt crisis. There is also a continuing need to manage demand that runs at 106–107% of income and output: an almost impossible task.
- Huge deflation of euro-zone demand as it bore the brunt of exchange rate adjustment against both the dollar and Asia at a time when the introduction of the euro and confused allocation of policy formation – indeed a complete absence of it in the case of foreign exchange rate policy. This meant that demand collapsed even more severely for three years than it need have, despite already inadequate policies.
- China lurched away from market-oriented development after a boom-bust that will leave it painfully exposed if (as is likely) a US

downswing hits it just when it seeks good growth ahead of the 2008 Olympics.

On the plus side must be mentioned at least two benefits, the second probably temporary and likely to be painfully reversed:

- Japan was helped in finally checking its apparently unstoppable downward deflationary spiral.
- America's appetite for consumption and house-price gains was satisfied by easy money. This was a substitute for sustaining growth with continued rebalancing of its international accounts via some export growth. Asian economies were happy to provide the US with credit – 'vendor financing' in effect – achieving development at the expense of, for the time being, effectively giving away the resulting product.

4

House prices and household dis-saving: the debt build-up

Simple borrowing growth has cut household savings rates throughout most of the developed world, starting with America, Britain and Australia, and followed by parts of continental Europe, especially Spain and France. In Japan the personal savings rate has also decreased, but not through borrowing: the chief cause has been a generation passing through the age of 65 and changing from high, late-career savers to low-saving pensioners. The rise of household borrowing has generally been in parallel with rapid growth of house prices. The huge flow of funds from the Asian surpluses has provided a liquidity base from which banks have been able to expand their business by lending against homes. This surge of buying power has driven up the price of these homes and raised borrowing power, in a virtuous circle. Easy monetary policies have been the immediate driver of this process. Much of the borrowing has been to finance consumption, hence the lower savings rates. Increased new housing investment has also been a significant feature.

The increase in house prices has chiefly reflected two factors:

Figure 11 **House prices**
1996 = 100

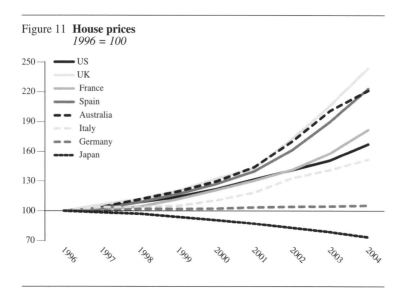

easy monetary policy to accommodate the Asian surpluses with current-account and domestic household deficits, as already outlined, and demographics. Thus Britain, with relatively easy monetary policies over the past seven or eight years and a strong flow of immigration to boost the labour force, has, along with Australia and Spain, had the largest house-price gains. Spanish prices have been boosted by easy money: the common euro interest rates (both short- and long-term) have been lower than Spanish inflation and therefore highly stimulative. France and the United States have lagged behind these three. In France, monetary policy and population trends probably boost house prices less than in America, but French house prices were notoriously low to start with. Italy, like Germany, suffers from a falling working-age population, but euro interest rates are far more stimulative in Italy (almost as much as in Spain) than in Germany. The result has been quite lively Italian house-price growth. In Japan all asset prices, including real estate, have been in a downward spiral from grossly excessive levels in its bubble (see below). Japan also suffered from the onset of a falling working-age population in the 1990s, before Germany and Italy.

House-price inflation took off after 2001, when interest rates were slashed in response to the recession. The phrase 'echo-bubble' gets its force from this handing over of the asset-price baton from the stockmarket in 1998–2000 to the housing market. While the idea of serial bubbles is an appealing metaphor for asset-price booms 'inflated' by the restless Asian surplus, the word bubble for an asset-price boom implies the expectation of a drastic fall when the 'bubble' is 'burst'. That seems unlikely to happen to house prices in the near future. House-price gains will be shown to be a much more logical and sustainable response to the Asian surpluses than stockmarket gains. But this has to be seen in a broad-brush global context as it has developed over the past 17 years.

In 1988, the developed world economy had settled down after the oil crises and a variety of early-1980s upheavals. But (as described at the start of this book) bolting onto the world economy the countries of the former Soviet Union, 1.25 billion Chinese and 1 billion Indians meant productive assets were suddenly in short supply relative to labour and potential labour. Prices of all assets therefore went up, but most of all those of productive assets. Hence the asset-price bubble initially (in the

1990s) was concentrated in the stockmarket (outside Japan). The huge extra supply of labour reinforced monetary stringency in cutting down inflation. So bond prices also gained mightily.

But growth in China and India, though rapid, is less impressive relative to their low level of incomes – i.e. large catch-up potential – and rates of capital investment. This is by comparison with European growth in the 1950s and 1960s, and Japan and South Korea in the 1960s and 1970s.[4] The savings glut is associated with and partly the result of this inadequate growth performance. A global shortage of productive assets, resulting in their prices rising, should have provoked faster development of Asian emerging economies. This should have involved higher consumer spending, given their poverty, as well as investment. It has not, and excessive savings are one result. So the boom in asset prices has switched naturally from productive assets (the stockmarket) to land (property or real estate) as these surpluses seek a home, aided by the gearing of cheaper debt.

In principle, lower interest rates favour most the prices of the longest-lasting assets, which ultimately means land. This argument can be developed either by examining property, real estate and land as investment assets, or by considering the position of a person intending to finance a purchase of a house with borrowed money. In either case, a fundamental point is that variations in the price of land are the chief element in variations of the price of real estate in general, or houses in particular. It is common to observe that the same house will have different values in, for example, London and rural Scotland: hence the property person's constant refrain 'location, location, location'.

Figure 12 **US household wealth**
As multiple of disposable income

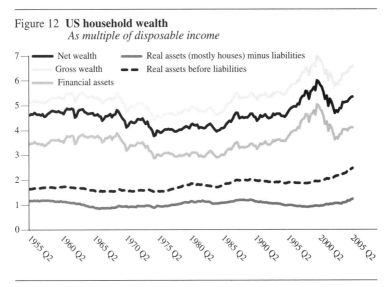

Likewise, variations over time in the cost of a house in a given place are generally only weakly connected to replacement, or building, costs. The remainder of such variation over time reflects movements in the value of the land (or location).

Viewed in terms of return on an investment asset, the rent on real estate is 'real' – i.e. inflation-protected – on the normal assumption that land at least holds its value in the long run. The real rate of interest, if falling, therefore provides a justification for lower rental rates. But if rental yields fall from 6% to 5%, for example, without any change in the actual cash rent being paid, the value of the real estate will increase by 6/5, or 20%. For example, imagine a property yielding £6,000 in rent. If rental yields are 6%, its value is £100,000. If rental yields fall to 5%, its value will go up to £120,000, as the £6,000 rent is 5% of

£120,000. £120,000 is of course 20% up from £100,000, a ratio of 6/5, the inverted change in rental rate.

In 1985–2000, the yield of long-term bonds decreased a lot because of lower inflation, but the real yield (nominal, or actual, yield minus inflation) stayed high, typically around 4–5% for US government debt. Two leveraged booms, end-1980s and end-1990s, saw to that. Also, the bond market scars from high inflation ensured that investors brought yields down 'behind' inflation, so that the yield differential above inflation, i.e. the real yield, remained high. High real yields meant real estate and housing did not do particularly well. But from 2001, real yields fell as stockmarkets crumbled and business worldwide shifted its finances from net borrowing to net lending. These conditions are highly favourable to real estate in general, specifically land prices, including housing.

Affordability

Perhaps an easier way to see why much higher house prices are justified is to look at the 'affordability' of borrowing to buy a house, i.e. the ability of people to afford the cost of a typical mortgage. Affordability reflects three phenomena: the income available to support a mortgage; the house price needing to be financed; and the interest rate and term of the mortgage. In effect, lower inflation and interest rates make long-lasting assets like houses more affordable, because they make genuinely long-term loans possible. For example, a £100,000 25-year loan at a 12%

rate of interest when inflation is 8% will lead to a payment of about £12,750 a year. Of the £12,750 in the first year, £8,000 is the inflation element in the interest rate, £4,000 is the 'real' interest element and £750 is the principal repayment. But while the lender is owed £99,250 in theory at the end of year one, in real terms (allowing for inflation) the value of the amount outstanding is 8% less than this. In effect, the £8,000 inflation element in the first year's payment was capital repayment: compensation to the lender for the effect of inflation on the principal value of the loan. But this large, immediate, inflation-adjusted reduction of the principal outstanding is a heavy burden for the borrower.

Take away excessive inflation, and affordability of loans improves. A loan bearing a 6% rate with inflation at 2% has the same 4% real interest rate. But the annual payment is only £7,820, nearly £5,000 less than in the 12% case. The capital repayment in year one is £3,820, inflation-adjusted for only 2% in this case, rather than £8,750 in the 12% loan example. The lower inflation and interest rate makes the repayment much less burdensome. If lower real interest rates are layered onto this, the position becomes even more favourable. With the same 2% inflation rate, a real interest rate of 2% (half the 4% real rate used so far) would mean a total interest rate payable of 4%. The £100,000 loan over 25 years then comes down in annual cost to £6,400. It is not hard to see why lower inflation followed by lower real interest rates has led to higher house prices. People can simply afford more.

In America, the National Association of Realtors computes its own affordability index, which is based on 100 when a family on the median income can just afford a mortgage on the going

Figure 13 **US and UK housing affordability indices**

━ US: National Association of Realtors affordability index: at 100, the household on median income can just afford the median-priced home at the going mortgage rate (lh scale)

━ UK: annual payment on average house price mortgaged at average mortgage rate over 25 years, versus average HH disposable income (rh scale)

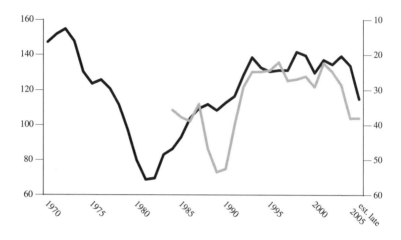

terms on a house at the median price. The going terms were much improved by lower interest rates in the period since the index started in 1981. The mortgage rate hit its high at over 16% in 1981–82, settled down at just over 10% in 1986–90, and then came down steadily through the 1990s to 7–8% in 1999–2000, and under 6% in 2003–04. Only recently has the acceleration of house-price inflation to the mid-teens brought affordability down to the level of 1990, and it remains above that of the 1980s.

In Britain, affordability is probably better at this point than in the United States. Looking at the mortgage cost (over 25 years) of the average house price for the average household income at the going rate of interest, or simply relating house prices and/or mortgage amounts taken out to the average incomes declared on application forms, the 2004 level of affordability is the same or slightly better than in 1984–87, and far better than in the bubble years of 1989–90. This appears to contradict the all-time record ratio of house prices to average earnings. But that ratio takes account neither of the reductions in mortgage interest rates (which helps affordability) nor of the increased number of incomes supporting the average mortgage. The increase in two-income mortgages means that today's average mortgage is supported by 1.6 incomes compared with 1.2 incomes 15 years ago. This raises house-price affordability relative to average earnings. Despite the large gains in UK house prices, affordability appears to compare quite favourably with the past.

Dangers of the debt burden

The danger in the debt-financed run-up of house prices lies not so much in the price levels so far achieved as in the debt burden taken on. Moreover, the new debt that has to be taken up each year for households to 'do their bit' in using up the Eurasian surplus may require that acceptable affordability now will not last, as house prices have to carry on up to keep households borrowing. This immediately removes continental Europe from the risk list. Whereas household liabilities relative to disposable income have shot up to 160% in Britain and 125% in the US, in continental

Europe only in Germany are they over 100%. Germany has no house-price inflation and very low short- and long-term interest rates: it is out of the 'borrow-and-spend' game, which is part of the savings glut problem, not the 'spend today, worry tomorrow' solution. In France, Italy and Spain household liabilities are in the region of 60% of disposable income. The reasons for this vary by country, but common features are very light use of housing debt to finance consumption, and, until recently, relatively primitive financial systems ill-adjusted to the needs of households rather than business (rather like the Asian developing countries although somewhat further on than them). Continental European housing debt is largely for house purchase, and is generally a smaller proportion of the house price with more arduous conditions. By contrast, the Anglo-Saxon world has used its housing collateral for equity withdrawal by means of refinancing mortgages at a higher level, as rates have come down, or by borrowing under second-mortgage facilities.

Vulnerability arising from high debt can take at least two forms, leaving aside loss of work or being obliged to take a lower-paying job. First, the relatively benign affordability analysis above is correct only in terms of the cash flow financing capacity of households confronted with higher house prices. It does not alter the fact that new debt burdens are real, and last longer in a non-inflationary environment. In the 1980s, new home-buyers might have been stretched to afford their monthly mortgage payments, but they could reflect that a few years of wage or salary increases at inflated rates would make those payments far less of a burden. In other words, the high initial effective repayment in inflationary

Figure 14 **US household debt measures**
% of disposable income

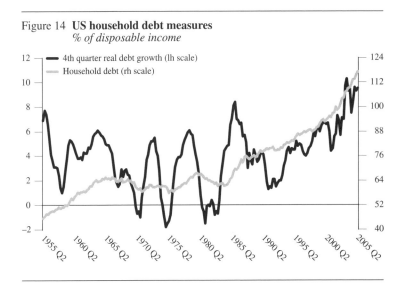

conditions had its corollary in later relief. This is a slow-burn drawback to taking on a 'full-stretch' mortgage in present conditions, but a real enough one. More immediately serious, of course, is that a high debt burden relative to income means that households are affected much more by increases in interest rates. And the impact of a 0.5% rise in rates will be proportionately much larger at low interest rates than high ones, even before allowing for the newly high debt ratio to income. In America, rising interest rates are an everyday reality.

Moreover, sustaining world demand, and preventing a depression resulting from the Asian savings excess, requires western households to continue each year to add debt and raise their debt/income ratio. US households have increased their real debt outstanding by just under 10% of disposable income for the past 2–3 years. (In nominal terms, the annual debt increase has been 12–13% of disposable income.) But the trend rate of US GDP growth, and therefore real income, is at or just above 3%. (Real income has grown faster recently because of tax cuts and the resulting boom, but further tax cuts to sustain such growth are not in prospect, given the scale of the budget deficit.) With household liabilities now 125% of disposable income, of which debt is nearly 120 percentage points, the increase of real debt is 8–9% of existing liabilities. Growth of liabilities at 8–9%, where real income is growing at only 3%, really is unsustainable. Yet that is what is required to keep the world economy on an even keel. Clearly, such growth in liabilities is only possible even in the short term as long as house prices boom – and boom they must until they are beyond affordability.

Before working out this iron logic – the anvil on which the world economy is likely to be broken – it is necessary to connect the western economic experience to that of China and the Tigers. Also, an understanding of the forces at work is enormously helped by looking at the Japanese experience, which since its bubble in 1989 has been a 'dry run' for many of the issues and problems addressed here.

5

Excess savings and Japan, 1989–2005: debt and pension shortfalls compounded

Japan's late-1980s bubble was followed by its 'long night of the '90s'. This gives some useful hints about the forces at work – it is no coincidence that Japan has been a major part of the current Eurasian surplus problem. There are major differences between Japan's particular experience and the global story in recent years. But there are also major points in common: lessons that can be learned by policymakers, if they so wish, and by anyone who wants to understand what is going on and what the future may hold. A crucial common point is that a structural excess of savings has been a large part of Japan's problems for the better part of 20 years.

Until the mid-1980s, Japan had a high personal (household) saving rate, but a conventional rate of business saving (i.e. depreciation plus retained profit). In the United States, for example, business savings have for the past 25 years been in the region of 12–13% of GDP. Japan's was just above this, but for a country with a trend growth rate of 5%, i.e. still in catch-up mode rather

Figure 15 **Japanese private saving**
% of GDP

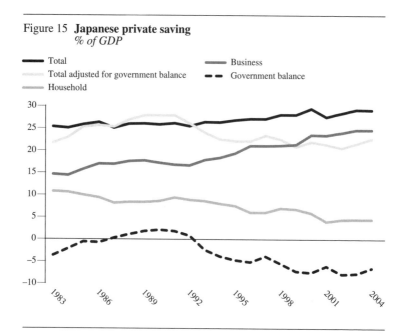

than a mature economy, it was not out of line. As the late 1980s bubble developed, this pushed upwards to around 17–18%. Household saving remained high. The boom boosted government tax receipts and its accounts went into surplus. The combination of private saving and government balance moved to 28% of GDP, an increase of 5–6 percentage points over 5–6 years.

This was excessive saving at the national level. Because the bubble involved – in fact was led by – strong business investment, industrial capacity soared. Excess capacity held down inflation. Monetary policy, with the Bank of Japan (BoJ) seeing little inflation, was not particularly tight. So the current-account surplus was not particularly large: the savings were being used in the home market for overinvestment. This provided a fairly clean analogy with the 1998–2000 US bubble, which was the first-round effect of excessive Asian savings after the Asian crisis ten years later.

As well as the similarities in the generation of the two bubbles – each reflecting huge liquidity expressing itself in asset prices and overinvestment rather than consumer price inflation – there was further similarity in the leveraging up of business with debt. But Japan's bubble was a lot more noxious than the 1998–2000 bubble for a number of reasons:

- As well as a stockmarket bubble, real estate prices reached ridiculous heights, to the extent that the Emperor's Palace was assessed to be worth more than California. In the long 1990–2003 bear market, real estate as well as stock prices fell by 80% or so.

- Japan's demographic trend was changing. From labour force growth in the 1980s, it slowed to stagnation and then a falling working-age population in the 1990s. This tended to increase (late-career) saving and simultaneously decrease capital spending needs, especially on construction. The excess saving, i.e. demand deficiency, was aggravated. This has been an early-2000s problem in Europe, but less so in America.

- The end of the 1980s marked the end of Japan's fast-growth catch-up development. The growth trend in the 1980s was just under 5%, well ahead of the United States and western Europe. In the 1990s, partly through the effects of the working-age population reversal, the long-run trend GDP growth rate fell dramatically to about 1%. This too is mirrored in the post-2000 euro zone, lower growth trends being associated, as in Japan, with the demographic downswing.

- The sharp fall in trend growth meant the old habit of loading firms with debt would not be justified by 'growing out of trouble'. And debt ratios in Japan in 1990 were in any case higher than in the United States ten years later.

- US policy took a year or two to react fully to the bubble bursting. Firms were restructuring hard by the end of 2001. But Japan was in denial from 1990 until 1996, during which time debt ratios and excess capacity got much worse.

- Japan's top-down, directed development system had worked quite well in securing catch-up growth, but proved a serious liability once economic maturity was achieved. The shift to a bottom-up, market-based system with firms aiming for shareholder value has been a big wrench. Again, the analogy is with core euro-zone countries since 2000, but not America.

Clearly, the US bubble was less serious than the one ten years previously in Japan, and the immediacy of action limited the damage. For example, between 1990 and 1997, when Japan finally took on the full challenge of its bubble, government debt rose from 60% to 100% of GDP, and the lurch into deficit had become chronic dependency. The reason for Japan's delay was that its bubble posed a far deeper challenge to Japanese society, politics and policymaking than the US bubble did. (We shall see later how elements of denial in present US society and policies are aggravating vulnerability to the Asian savings glut.)

Japan in 1990 was a consensus-driven, top-down, collectivist society, economy and polity. Brian Reading, who wrote a path-breaking book called *Japan, the Coming Collapse* in 1991, called it 'not capitalism with warts, but communism with beauty spots'. Business pursued sales, not profits. Workers enjoyed the lifetime employment system, in which they were tied to employers, and benefited from firm-level pensions, health and social security, mortgages and housing, and of course salaries and bonuses. The corrupt nexus of the Liberal Democratic Party (LDP), the bureaucracy and locally based real estate interests, bound together by the tradition of Cabinet-level unanimity policed by the civil service, sorted out the spoils at both the national and local level. Business looked to Japan Inc for the direction of policy.

When the bubble burst, the various Japanese interests thought it was simply a particularly nasty cyclical experience. Businesses did not realise that future gains in output and incomes would require decision-making reoriented to profit maximisation and shareholder value, if the legacy of gross excess capacity and debt were to be worked off. This point was strengthened by the end of easy catch-up growth and the need for market forces and price signals to drive decisions once the economy was no longer simply imitating America, but operating near the technological frontier. Initially, Japanese companies cut capital spending sharply and simply waited for growth to revive. But the excess saving was structural. With business capital expenditure cut to 15% of GDP (still well above the US level, despite America's faster growth) and with housing trimmed back sharply by population slowdown, and the private savings rate edging upward from 26% to 29% of GDP, there was a chronic deficiency of demand.

The adjustment route chosen was a continuation of previous habits, without the change of behaviour that was needed. A surge of government investment projects provided the 'iron triangle' of LDP politicians, bureaucrats and local business people with huge spoils to share. And the spending was needed as a Keynesian deficit boost to demand to avoid what would probably otherwise have been a slump or depression. By 1995, interest rates had been lowered close to zero (there to remain) as the yen spiked to a peak in the low 80s against the dollar. (It quickly fell back to over 100, and has remained there ever since.) Alongside low (to zero) interest rates, the government's shift into a deficit of 5% of GDP was also crucial to sustaining demand. As the yen fell back, some growth revived into early 1997. For a while, Japanese businesses may have thought the worst was over.

At that point the government decided to claw back towards budget balance with tax increases. This was much criticised at the time, but looks correct in retrospect. As it turned out, the Asian crisis starting several months later affected Japan as well, but what was less appreciated was that even with only modest growth the economy was 3–4% overheated in spring 1997. This was because the sustainable long-run trend growth rate had fallen so far, from 5% in the 1980s to 1% in the 1990s, that only a mild growth recovery by past standards took the economy over the 'speed limit'. The time for addressing the true societal, political and supply-side issues had arrived.

Sadly, in the six or seven wasted years, as well as a much higher government debt burden, Japan's businesses had raised their debt from under six times gross operating cash flow (depreciation plus pre-interest profit) to just under seven times. The mountain to be climbed was higher and steeper. The makings of the banking crisis were in place. To get the matter in perspective, if a firm has debt of five times its gross cash flow its debt is considered junk. The US non-financial sector reached a collective ratio of 4.25–4.5 times at the post-bubble peak in mid-2001 (if official data are adjusted by adding back in off-balance-sheet debt supporting operating assets in Enron-style partnerships – much of American business's real estate, tracks, cars and trade receivables had been taken off balance sheets in this way in the 1990s). That meant perhaps one-third of the firms were above five and therefore junk. For the Japanese non-financial sector to be collectively on nearly seven times was dire. The cure was seven years of deflation.

The remainder of the story is of how Japan has remained chronically short of demand because of the violent restructuring needed to put right the acute financial conditions. In effect, Japan Inc was bust, internally, vis-à-vis its bank and household creditors; the external side showed a plenitude of overseas assets. In 2004, jobs had fallen by 0.5% a year for seven years; average pay had been carved up even more, falling 1.25% on average each year for seven years. Two recessions, in 1998 and 2001, formed part of this. The increase in business cash flow was tremendous. Its saving moved up even further than before to 25% of GDP – astonishingly nearly twice the US rate of business saving (which is itself quite strong). In cash terms, the money saved was not spent in any way but used to repay debt: this shortfall of demand was brutal debt deflation. In accounting terms, the major gains in operating profits were wiped out by provisions for depleted pension funds, losses on real estate holdings and cross-holdings of shares, much of Japanese business being plagued by old collectivist mutual ownership arrangements. By 2002 the worst was over, and the economy started a good recovery, though it was only in 2005 that labour income started to grow and house prices stabilised – probably at last presaging a boom.

What is the relevance of all this to the rest of us? In terms of the aftermath of the 1998–2000 bubble, the principal factors are the differences. But the Japanese experience gives an awful warning of the dangers of delusion and denial. Willing acceptance of much higher levels of indebtedness by governments and households has permitted a surprisingly robust growth path since 2002 in America and Britain, and 2004 in continental Europe. But the resulting burden of debt carries serious future risks, particularly when set against two other features of the financial landscape:

- **The absence of inflation.** This means that debts now have to be repaid out of real income, rather than inflated away as in 1965–95. The probable US downswing as the household borrow-and-spend game is played out and exhausted could take inflation down to very low levels, if not quite the falling prices experienced in Japan.
- **Population ageing.** The future will require the working part of the population and its capital to support much larger burdens than in the past, owing to the much increased proportion of older, retired people. Expressed in financial terms, this is like saying the obligation to pay pensions to future pensioners is a much larger propor-

tion of national income than has been true in the past. Add to this a huge pile of government and household debt inherited from battling the post-bubble torpor – or, put another way, combating excessive Asian savings – and the resources available for active members of the population could be curtailed. But of course the reduced ratio of such active people will give them greater bargaining power in offering their labour, which in normal economic logic should lead to higher, not lower, real incomes.

The result may be high real incomes for working people, but prolonged comparative poverty for the numerous old people. This could occur both directly, via inadequate resources to pay pensions, and via shrinking profit incomes as high real labour pay – plus extra taxes levied by government to finance pensioners, who would use their voting power – cuts into the flow of funds that normally goes into interest and dividend payments.

Probably the most important difference between Japan and the United States is that the US bubble did not affect real estate and house prices much. Tax cuts to stimulate US consumer spending were therefore easily reinforced by household borrowing at the Fed's much lowered short-term rates as house prices had plenty of scope to increase. In effect, while Japan had simultaneous bubbles in stocks and real estate, the United States (and Britain, Australia, Spain and even France) have been able to bring property price inflation into action as a second round of asset-price stimulus, via easy monetary policy – the 'echo-bubble' referred to earlier. Analysis of the affordability of new, higher house prices does not support the idea that they are a bubble. The much lower interest rates now prevailing are beneficial more than anything else to housing finance and land prices. The echo-bubble idea achieves its true resonance on the debt side. By 1997, Japan had a personal sector with huge net assets and low debt; but business and increasingly government were crippled with debt that took seven lean years to get back adequately towards balance. By 2005, America and Britain had business sectors with perfectly satisfactory balance sheets. But households and increasingly governments are taking on debt that could cripple the economy in future.

The Japanese experience points to the huge dangers, not on the asset side of the balance sheet but on the liability side. It is not just coincidence that Japan went through the shift into falling working-age population some ten years earlier than the West, with its baby-boomer age-group peak now, and also had its bubble ten years earlier. The debt deflation that plagued Japan when it finally faced up to its problems from 1997 onwards was also accompanied by massive provisions to restore the adequacy of pension funds, and, in a number of Japanese companies, simple arbitrary cuts in the pensions being paid – an early hint of pensioner poverty risks.

No country is more blatantly in denial about pension finance than America. As well as the issue of baby-boomers' 'inverted Alzheimer's disease', the provision for companies' pension liabilities under US accounting rules encourages their understatement for the benefit of current shareholders. Many firms are now borrowing heavily to buy back their own stock on that basis and thereby shrinking the capital base of the economy. These liabilities seriously sap the ability of the system to deal with an economic downswing, which is forecast probably for 2006, maybe later. As the burden of debt and future pensions is raised first by higher interest rates and later by demand deflation, it could keep the economy depressed for years.

6

The dénouement: liquidity trap in 2006–07

The longer-term risks to America (and potentially Britain) from building up debt to 'use up' excess Asian savings are likely to be short-circuited by a cyclical downturn. What could make it worse for the United States is that the Federal Reserve's policy was reactive in the bubble and in the subsequent hard landing, and remains so now. US interest rate adjustments were 'too much, too late' in the 1998–2000 bubble, and then again in the downswing. This pattern has now been repeated in the 2003–05 upswing. In the euro zone, demand management overall was also deflationary between 2001 and 2003. Now the fiscal ease in France and Italy, combined with stimulative monetary effects there and in Spain from the common euro interest rates, is not merely 'too much, too late' but is likely to blow up the still-immature euro zone itself. To be precise, it could eventually force the weaker members to leave. America could experience a hard landing in 2006–07, and the euro zone could break up later in the decade.

In the discussion of the New Dollar Area (see Chapter 3), the sheer short-term convenience of the current set-up was raised. Americans enjoy consuming more than their output or income. China is happy to oblige with trade credit. This arrangement was not entered into voluntarily by the United States, but it has gone along with it willingly so far. Free trade has been extremely good for aggregate incomes in all countries, and for helping the poor in China and elsewhere in Asia climb up from the bottom of the income ladder. The concomitant capital gains and low interest rates have enabled even poorer Americans, whose labour has lost bargaining power, to borrow against their appreciating house prices or – for those who are not yet owners – to afford a mortgage. For better-off Americans it has been a bonanza: large rises in income associated with capital, real estate and its management; huge capital gains; and major tax cuts largely for the benefit of those on high (and relatively rising) incomes. These benign conditions are the chief reason the Bush administration easily achieved re-election in November 2004. Not unnaturally, measures to curb China's undue gains of competitiveness and to make the painful cuts in US consumption needed to reduce the external financial imbalance have been kept firmly in the realm of discussion rather than action.

This Sino-US synergy is not a formal arrangement and certainly not marriage (like EMU). It is not even agreed cohabitation. It is as if China has simply moved into the basement and taken over as servant. The danger of such arrangements was illustrated by *The Servant* (a Harold Pinter play made into a film by Joseph Losey in 1963), in which the master continued to go out into society as the man of the world, while in the home a role reversal took place:

his increasing dependence on the servant transferred true power to the latter. As long as China can dress up its own convenience to match the immediate interests of America, this process may continue. But the United States will quite soon discover the true costs of its policy, and the adjustment could be abrupt, both in domestic attitudes and in tolerance of China's mode of economic development.

There are at least three stress points in the Sino-US synergy:

- The increase of US household debt beyond viable limits, as discussed earlier.

- The loss of relative income (even absolute real income in many cases) by the poorer part of the population, whose bargaining power as labour is drastically undermined by globalisation. To illustrate the skewing of the distribution of income, consider that the average ('mean') real disposable income of the US personal sector rose in 2004 by an unusually large 5% per head. However, the median real household income fell slightly. The median is the level at which half the people have more and half have less. This combination of rising mean and falling median can only occur if relatively few incomes at the top are rising quite fast, and the majority at the bottom are falling. This is the natural result of globalisation forces within a free market economy such as America's (and few others). It has been reinforced by the Bush tax cuts, which almost exclusively favour the well-off.

- Head-on competition, rather than synergy, in demand for oil. This is not true of most energy and raw materials, for which the United States has a rapidly declining marginal appetite, but it will always be true for oil, as long as anything remotely approaching current US driving habits remains in place.

When it comes to oil, the effects are pretty concrete. China's demand for oil is 6.5 million barrels a day (mbpd) compared with over 20 mbpd for the United States and just under 50 mbpd for the OECD. But China has an 8–9% growth rate. And its oil demand tends to increase 1% for every 1% of GDP growth. So its incremental oil demand each year is over 0.5 mbpd. Other developing Asian countries (excluding Middle Eastern countries, which are mostly OPEC) have oil demand of 8.5 mbpd, reflecting the emergence of India. A similar 1-for-1 relationship of their oil demand growth to their average GDP growth of 6% means the incremental demand is the same as China's, so total incremental growth for developing Asia total is over 1 mbpd. But the OECD has only 0.4% oil demand growth for every 1% of GDP increase, because developed country growth is concentrated in service industries that use few material resources. So incremental OECD oil demand each year, given trend growth of only 2–2.5%, is a little less than 0.5 mbpd, half that of developing countries in Asia. With growing demand in other parts of the world, incremental oil demand is now some 2.25 mbpd, compared with only 1.25 mbpd as recently as ten years ago. Such is the impact of Asian emergence.

The bulk of the OECD's incremental demand is for gasoline in the United States. So the interests of American consumers are not so aligned with developing Asia's as might appear at first sight. Nor will the situation get any easier in the medium term. On the supply side, just over one-third of the world's 84–85 mbpd comes from OPEC and two-thirds from the rest of the world. But in the North Sea, output is depleting, as it is in Alaska and the other US states, and it is topping out in Canada (excluding the Athabasca tar sands) and Mexico. Russia's oil sector is being damaged by state control and crude policies (as in the 1980s), and output from other former Soviet-Union countries is hardly soaring. The rest of the world is increasing output a bit, but reliance on OPEC – which means the Gulf states, where the greater part of known reserves is located – is rising fast. To call this situation strategically lethal is an understatement.

Sino-US stress points take their toll

The hurricanes that battered America in 2005 – Katrina especially, but Rita and Wilma too – seriously exacerbated the three stress points mentioned above. With regard to oil, the cut-off of Mexican Gulf production may well be less important than the loss of 5% of US refining capacity in New Orleans. With the world short of refining capacity in any case, Katrina jerked up US gasoline prices by 20–25% in spite of European strategic reserve releases, especially by Germany. Oil's role as a stress point was sharpened.

When it comes to the distribution of income, the role of Katrina is less immediate, but probably more far-reaching. The lid was lifted from America's 'left-behinds'. This was literally true of New Orleans inhabitants fleeing the hurricane, but also metaphorically, in the sense of the whole bottom swathe of

American society being left behind by globalisation and tax cuts largely concentrated on those with high incomes. The Bush administration added insult to injury by its apparently complete indifference to the emergency for a crucial few days, followed by the simple incompetence of an unqualified appointee to the relevant federal agency.

A crisis in the United States over free trade could occur at any time, when the Chinese surplus continues to grow, even explode, at the point when American consumers are hit by higher interest rates. Rebalancing of US overseas accounts, when it comes, will lead to a cut in domestic spending from 106–107% of output and incomes to something closer to 100%. In such situations people do not blame themselves, and in this case the easy target will be China. Attacks on globalisation and free trade are inevitable from opponents of the current US government, as proxies for (understandable) attacks on its tax policies.

The hurricane damage is likely to mean that monetary policy, paradoxically, will be tightened faster. Federal government spending will be the chief means of financing the rebuilding of the huge affected areas. The government's being discredited means it is likely to throw money at the problem. As it happens, shifting demand patterns of US consumer spending – not being dim, consumers are (since Katrina) buying fewer gas-guzzlers and less gasoline – are holding up the volume of spending, as people switch to buying things that are less plagued by rising prices. Meanwhile, the move back towards increasing the budget deficit means rapidly growing demand. The Fed is likely to take the view that looser fiscal policy should mean tighter monetary policy – higher interest rates sooner. So the tipping point at which household debt becomes intolerable has come closer.

The rest of the world is not standing still. The Asian surplus is redistributing itself. The handling of the huge Asian reserve build-up is also changing. In effect, the counterpart surplus to the US deficit is becoming less structural and more cyclical. It is also becoming dangerously concentrated in China, so that American anxiety about the rise of China will readily lead to political attacks when the going gets tough.

In 2004, the Eurasian structural surplus was $730 billion; this fell by nearly $200 billion to $540 billion if western Europe as a whole was included, not just the central-northern structural surplus countries centred round Germany. In 2005, the Eurasian total was estimated to have grown to $830 billion, partly because of higher Russian oil export revenues, which are cyclical, reflecting excess demand, not structural, threatening deficient demand. But the total including the whole of western Europe rather than just north-central Europe is only up to $575 billion, as deficits have grown fast in Mediterranean Europe. Meanwhile, as well as oil revenue gains boosting Russia's surplus, the surplus of other oil exporters (including OPEC) was expected to increase by $100 billion in 2005 to $150 billion. So there are two phenomena:

- Within Europe, imbalances are increasing between the sustained north-central surplus and the growing deficits in the Mediterranean region.
- Treating western Europe as a whole, the world is seeing a roughly sustained level of structural surplus – now properly called the Asian,

rather than Eurasian, savings glut – with a much increased overall imbalance owing to oil exporters' gains (and growing deficits, chiefly in America).

Concerning the lower US bond yields resulting from the Asian savings excess, Tim Congdon, a celebrated British economist and former colleague, recently asked: 'What happens when the surpluses go away?' That will no doubt happen at some stage, but not yet. However, a cyclical, oil-producer surplus is a symptom of excess demand: exactly the opposite of the structural Asian surplus. Unlike the structural surpluses that reflect a deficiency of demand, these surpluses arise from Sino-US competition for oil. Increasingly, oil-exporters' surpluses will further increase demand as they spend the money on imports. The shift of surpluses toward this cyclical element may imply higher bond yields.

It is impressive that the structural surplus in north-central Europe – Germany, Benelux, Scandinavia, Switzerland and Austria – is little changed, despite higher oil prices. Germany's quintuple deflation (exchange rate, fiscal, monetary, restructuring and demographic) has created such rapidly increasing competitiveness that it offsets extra oil costs. But these exports are to a large degree at the expense of Italy, Spain, Portugal and Greece, where rapid demand growth nurtures lower-cost, central-northern European exporters, who are gaining market share. The EU's balance of payments overall, including Britain, which runs a deficit, and the recent east-central EU entrants, shifted by $100 billion at an annual rate between early and late 2005. Of this huge change, about half reflects higher oil costs and the rest real increases of imports ahead of exports. So the Eurasian savings excess we have spoken of has become Ben Bernanke's 'Asian savings glut'.

The expansion of demand in Europe, and the resulting fall in its overall surplus, takes it out of the global argument over financial imbalances. But within the euro zone the imbalances are rapidly increasing. It is one thing for German labour cost deflation to eliminate its overvaluation at the inception of EMU in 1999. It is quite another for Italian and Spanish costs now to continue growing by 3% or so faster than Germany's. The effect is that lack of export competitiveness forces Italy and Spain to rely increasingly on domestic demand for growth, with rapidly increasing trade deficits. Certainly in Italy already, and probably in Spain once the current hectic real estate boom lapses, this domestic demand growth requires growing government deficits. In Italy, government debt is already over 100% of GDP. The permanently fixed exchange rates between EMU countries (its chief feature) mean these imbalances can be expected to grow, unless the Mediterranean countries at some point engage in drastic deflation. It is unlikely that they will do so as readily as Germany in 2001–04. So the current mechanism of euro-zone growth will probably require at least Italy to fall out of EMU within a few years. (For Spain, Portugal and Greece, the issue is less clear, as faster labour-cost growth may be offset by them starting from a much lower level, unlike Italy.)

Meanwhile in Japan, domestic demand is growing. Labour income is finally increasing, after falling for seven years, and household confidence is further boosted by the end of major house-

Table 2 **China's exploding current-account surplus**

	2004	2005	2006	2007	2008	2009	2010
$ billion							
Exports	593	771	964	1,205	1,507	1,883	2,354
Slow imports	561	656	787	945	1,134	1,360	1,632
Fast imports	561	656	820	1,025	1,281	1,602	2,002
Invisibles	35	35	35	35	35	35	35
Current-account balance ($ billion)							
Slow imports	**68**	**151**	**212**	**296**	**408**	**558**	**757**
Fast imports	**68**	**151**	**180**	**216**	**261**	**317**	**388**
Annual growth (%)							
Exports	–	30	25	25	25	25	25
Imports (slow)	–	17	20	20	20	20	20
Imports (fast)	–	17	25	25	25	25	25

price deflation. The surplus is little changed, as growing imports and higher oil costs are offset by buoyant exports, stimulated by the global boom, especially in America. Among the Asian Tigers, there is a more muted revival of domestic demand, and a greater impact of the slowdown of exports to China (their most important market) as well as the impact of oil prices. For China and the Tigers, the increase of oil prices in 2005 cost about 3% of GDP (from 5% to 8%). In China's case this effect is dampened in the short term by price controls and domestic production (also price-controlled) of about 40% of its demand. For other Tigers, such price controls as exist are less benign, severely affecting industrial behaviour as well as consumer thrift in response to world shortage. So Asian Tiger surpluses are reducing somewhat.

China's surplus, however, is exploding, despite higher oil import costs. Exports continued to rise at more than 30% in 2005 (only temporarily held back by the so-called EU 'bra wars'). But imports are up by only 15–17%, including the effect of higher oil prices. This could raise the current surplus from 2004's $70 billion by some $80 billion in 2005 to $150 billion (over 8% of GDP). Without higher oil prices 2005's surplus would approach $200 billion. On modest assumptions for the future, China's surplus will rise to $400 billion by 2010. It does not take extravagant assumptions to get that projection to twice that level, which would be a quarter of 2010's probable GDP. This would not be tolerated. And we know who will be first not to tolerate it. Although Europe has a less strong politico-intellectual tradition in favour of free trade than the United States, it has no serious mechanism for sustained obstruction of imports, outside the Common Agricultural Policy (which mostly hits African countries, not fast-growth Asia). But the US Congress has already voted for a huge tariff on Chinese imports and will probably soon revive the proposal if and when the pain level increases.

This rapid shift of the Asian surplus to China is no surprise, given its leading role in ensuring excessive Asian competitiveness via the yuan–dollar peg. But it helps take the focus off the US deficit and place it squarely on China's surplus, rather than some diffuse Eurasian structural problem. Meanwhile, the other increases in surplus counterparts to the US deficit are cyclical: much greater OPEC and Russian/former-Soviet-Union surpluses. The latter will dissipate over time. Either oil prices will fall, or these countries' imports will rise. So the cyclical forces are in favour of excess demand. In 2005, only China had slower domestic demand growth. Demand is accelerating in Europe, Japan, the Asian Tigers (mildly) and oil exporters. It is also accelerating in the United States, where unabated capital gains are ensuring capital-gains-related income growth as well as rampant household credit growth, at the same time as the federal government is borrowing to finance post-hurricane rebuilding.

Mercantilist China: exchange rate policy on the defensive

China's 2% revaluation of the yuan in July 2005, from 8.28/$ to 8.11/$, was the first, badly executed step down a long road. The explosion of the Chinese surplus had already put close observers – most obviously Asian central banks – on notice that the yuan would have to appreciate mightily in the relatively near term. China's half-baked blunder told them it would be done reluctantly, defensively and incompetently. At this stage, given the excessive domestic boom of 2003–04 resulting from China's mercantilist exchange rate policy, no reasonable shift in the yuan will do much to slow the growth of exports. The marginal labour cost of exports is small, once industrial capacity has been installed (excessive capacity in the Chinese case). Labour costs are especially small in China, which is why so much capacity has been installed there. If the exchange rate is raised by 25%, say, the extra yuan cost of labour will still leave it profitable at the margin to export. The revenue from exports will still greatly exceed their marginal cost, since a large part of the total cost is the sunk cost of the original capital investment. This is particularly true in energy and materials-intensive China, where the yuan cost of dollar-priced imported energy and materials will become lower after an appreciation of the yuan. So even the marginal costs of production are in many cases diminished by currency appreciation.

The combination of continued rapid Chinese surplus growth under almost any exchange rate scenario is likely to prove a red rag to the US congressional bull. With the president's authority much reduced, and congressional elections looming at the end of 2006, the first of the three stress points in the Sino-US synergy to be tested could be the damage from globalisation to the American poor. The growing Chinese surplus is a monthly reminder of the pressure on their jobs and incomes. American politicians in general do not make the link between globalisation and the Asian surpluses on the one hand, and the capital gains and cheap debt enjoyed by most Americans on the other. They ascribe these mostly to their own merits, and largely focus on the downside of Asian economic emergence. After Katrina, and given the obscurity of China's policymaking and the defensive incompetence of its exchange rate management, the public argument in America is dominated by aggressive anti-Chinese rhetoric. So far, fairly moderate textile trade restrictions are all that have resulted, but much worse is quite likely. Even these restrictions, by inhibiting freedom of supply, are clearly inflationary in implication.

The other two stress points in Sino-US synergy are energy and raw material prices, and US household debt. Both are affected by the increasing breadth and strength of the world boom. Taking energy first, the upward pressure on prices has to remain strong until US growth is clearly slowing. To be sure, the upward spike of oil and refined product prices after Katrina has been duly reversed, but the forces behind rising prices have not gone away. This is not just a matter of the medium-term demand growth and supply constraints discussed earlier. It is also true in the short-term cyclical sense, as long as US growth continues. European and Japanese growth is not the problem. But China's domestic demand and GDP slowdown from early 2004 to early 2005 is being temporarily reversed by the sheer force of its export growth. China's oil demand in early 2005 was actually down from early 2004, as slower growth was reinforced by working off oil inventory built up in 2003–04. Its oil demand could now pick up as growth continues. Only a US downswing would slow the exports that are China's mainspring, but US growth is accelerating. The Chinese benefit from this knocks on to the oil-intensive Tigers too. Upward pressure on oil prices should soon reassert itself.

The US expansion is now broadly based and no longer largely dependent on household spending stimulated by tax cuts and low interest rates. Business capital spending has steady momentum, growing at high single-figure rates, as is housing. As well as consumers continuing to spend, the government has to respond to rebuilding needs in areas ravaged by hurricanes. Businesses cut inventories in mid-2005 but are now likely to build them up again to supply growing demand. On top of all this, the recovering demand of Europe and Japan is stimulating exports, aided by the US cost benefits of three years of dollar devaluation. As a result, in volume terms, for all the trade deficit problems with China, US exports are outstripping imports for the first time in years, resulting in a gain in net exports. For the past few years, negative net exports have cut 0.5–0.75% a year from domestic demand – this is part of the Sino-US synergy by which demand increases without inflationary pressure. Now, in a major switch, net exports may be adding some 0.5%.

Ironically, it is the removal of worsening US trade volumes that most threatens an economic hard landing in the near term, as opposed to a crippling long-run debt build-up if recent imbalances were to persist. Added to the pressure of domestic demand already growing at more than 4%, about 1% above the 'speed limit' (the 3% long-run sustainable potential growth rate), it means growth could accelerate towards 5%. The Fed is likely to be raising short-term US interest rates until well into 2006. They could reach 5% by the summer of 2006. In addition, the upswing in Europe and Japan, meaning much broader demand growth globally than when it was concentrated in America and Britain, is putting upward pressure on longer-term rates and bond yields.

US household debt: the weak link in 2006–07

This highlights the most important of the three stress points in Sino-US synergy: the potentially ruinous build-up of US household debt it entails. Much higher debt burdens give the Fed a significantly harder task in slowing the economy. At the moment, apart from exports (which remain relatively small at little over

10% of GDP), US growth depends ultimately on capital gains. These account for more than half the growth of labour income (via stock option exercise, real estate commissions, bonuses, and the like). They also underpin the willingness to borrow – and it is only by US households raising their real debt burden by 10% a year that consumer demand is kept from falling back relative to income. In other words, as well as providing half the growth of labour income, capital gains are essential to the net savings rate staying at zero – without which consumer spending would fall short of income. But at some stage the rise in interest rates and bond yields is likely to have two interactive effects. It will:

- reduce the affordability of housing loans, thereby curbing credit growth;
- reduce buyers' willingness to pay higher house prices.

But lower capital gains will mean the capital-related part of labour income – stock option gains, real estate commissions and bonuses – falls rather than rises. At that point total labour income growth will be less than conventional payrolls, normal pay excluding stock options, and so on. However, conventional payrolls are growing at only 3%. As and when that becomes the ceiling for total labour income growth, real labour incomes will have stopped growing, given inflation of 2–3%. That is exactly the stage at which household debt will start to feel burdensome, with income growth falling and interest costs rising. Housing affordability by then will be distinctly less. So the savings rate will rise just at the point that income is slowing. This double whammy is what the Fed rightly fears when it talks of deflationary risks being greater than inflationary ones. It is right, but the situation is not under control. The mode of expansion of the United States in the past three years, becoming dependent on vendor financing from Asia, has made this type of hard landing ineluctable.

A mitigating factor is that better European and Japanese growth should help export demand and soften the rebalancing away from 6–7% deficits. But there is an iron logic to this, too. US GDP is at or rather above its 'potential', i.e. a touch overheated. There is no scope for permitting net export rebalancing without cutting the ratio of domestic demand to GDP (i.e. income), which is now 106–107%. GDP is already above potential so extra GDP growth is not an escape route. It is domestic demand that has to adjust downwards. Exports may grow, holding up employment, but in that case real disposable income, and real spending per head, must be cut. In the absence of tax increases to reduce spending power, this can probably be achieved only by a major cyclical downswing – led by much reduced real income related to capital gains – and by sharp cuts in credit to households. The monetary policy process was described in the previous paragraph.

This snapping shut of the Asian glut liquidity trap is likely to be soon, in late 2006 or 2007. But US households have not been prepared for the idea that they cannot consume 6–7% more than they produce. It is regarded as an entitlement. Those at the lower end of the income scale will look around for someone to blame, and, as seen in past and present Democratic Party rhetoric, it will be China and/or globalisation, a.k.a. 'outsourcing'. In fact, large US income gains have been made possible by free importation of cheap goods from Asia. Any attempt to restrict imports will increase average costs and decrease average real incomes, making the drop in living standards that much more severe. But the switch to a US downswing will probably occur against the provocative backdrop of a soaring Chinese export surplus. At best, the result will be a huge yuan revaluation with substantial upward moves of the yen and the euro. In that case US exports would do well, and adjustment could be quite rapid, provided that either taxes were raised or monetary tightness was maintained. Political unpopularity is inevitable under any likely scenario. But the danger is that the US commitment to free trade and globalisation proves shallow. In that case a much deeper crisis will ensue.

As always in making gloomy predictions, the question must be confronted: supposing they are wrong. If the structural surplus does not shrink quite rapidly, growth might be maintained for several years on the recent pattern, with Asia continuing to underwrite cheap US and European borrowing. This is the 'denial' option, with likely consequences similar to Japan's (see Chapter 5). Essentially, the build-up of western debt to Asia will collide with the crystallisation of the baby-boomers' pension problem – those born in 1946 reaching 65 in 2011. The problem boils down to an almost Socratic dilemma: either the Asian surplus is sharply reduced quite soon, or it is not. If it is, the United States must accept a major income cut in the next couple of years, almost certainly involving a hard landing or recession. If it is not, growth will be blighted for years from 2009–10, and the baby-boomers' poverty trap will become a reality.

PART II

DIANA CHOYLEVA

7

China heads for a hard landing

China is a developing economy with an underdeveloped financial system. It has expanded tremendously over the past 25 years, but without tackling the extreme inefficiency of its mainly state-owned banking sector. The structure of the economy is such that once macroeconomic policy is relaxed, the result has invariably been the accumulation of excess capacity. Leaving the huge domestic savings in the hands of state banks, which lend mainly to state firms without being governed by market principles, encourages a colossal waste of productive resources during each boom. Overinvestment makes the downswings violent. Boom–busts have been the order of the day in China. The only exception in the current cycle is that now Chinese economic developments have a global reach.[5]

China has not tried to create national champions as Japan and South Korea did by cutting off foreign competition. But neither has it fostered a productive environment for companies to thrive in for the long term. Even the most entrepreneurial managers focus only on the short term. Fads are followed religiously, exacerbated by centuries of provincial rivalry. Often foreign investors only add to the investment bubbles. It is paradoxical that China, which has tremendous long-term potential, can so far offer investors only arbitrary short-term rewards.

After the Asian financial crisis and in response to the US downturn in 2000, the Chinese authorities eased fiscal and monetary policy substantially. With unlimited access to cheap credit and state guarantees, both local governments and state firms embarked on a massive spending spree, with little regard for return on capital. Private firms had to battle with unfair competition. Profit margins have been squeezed by output price deflation from overcapacity and by input price inflation from excess demand for commodities. Investment in manufacturing and real estate led the boom, while government-directed investment in infrastructure and energy fell behind. The combination of over-investment and overheating has made the economy vulnerable to the swings of the business cycle.

On the market side of the economy, when demand falters there will be hardly any need for investment growth. Investment could well fall. On the state side of the economy, politics rules. The long-term goal of the Communist Party has always been for the private sector to outgrow the public sector and eventually to eclipse it. But the state sector has not withered away, as short-term efforts to avoid the global cycle have gone against China's long-term goal. The authorities have always tried to perform a fine balancing act between high inflation and weak growth. They may wish to boost public investment further, if private investment falters, but at this point in the cycle if they continue to do so on the same scale as before, the economy will continue to overheat.

The overheating of the economy has manifested itself in severe energy and transport shortages. In 2004, 24 of the 31 Chinese provinces experienced regular blackouts and brownouts. The authorities administer the price of energy and have not let price movements function to balance supply and demand for energy.

China has realised the dangers of overinvestment. A series of restrictive administrative measures was introduced during 2004 and in early 2005. Policy tightening and overheating combined to induce a cyclical domestic demand slowdown. Chinese data are notoriously unreliable, making it difficult to pinpoint the timing of cyclical peaks and troughs. The politically correct annual real GDP growth figures understate the true magnitude of the swings, on both the downside and the upside. The experience of other developing economies, notably South Korea, suggests that these countries have violent business cycles. Chinese nominal GDP data are more trustworthy and show a Chinese cycle which is more volatile than the real growth numbers suggest.

The Chinese expansion peaked at nominal growth rates of 18% in the middle of 2004. By the autumn of 2005 output growth had slowed to around trend, estimated at around 11% in nominal terms. But within the total, domestic demand growth has weakened sharply. This is visible in the slowdown of import growth, the collapse of non-financial sector credit growth and significantly weaker foreign direct investment (FDI) inflows. However, buoyant world demand and an undervalued currency have continued to fuel rapid export expansion. Moreover, the low wage costs to total costs ratio suggests that businesses have the incentive to continue to produce even at a loss. Winding down production will result in even bigger losses. Buoyant export income has supported consumer spending.

However, external demand, the last bastion of growth, is likely to falter in 2006, as the US economy lands with a bump, led by slumping consumer spending. The Chinese, having used their domestic ammunition to fight the world economic slowdown at the start of this decade, could do little to counteract it this time round, especially given their already ballooning current-account surplus. Weak exports and an investment meltdown will hurt consumer spending. Lack of proper social security and pension safety nets and limited financial products to channel savings between generations suggests that consumer spending is unlikely to take up the baton.

A recession should not follow, but growth could be well below trend. The Chinese locomotive has been heading for a brick wall for some time. Currently, economic fundamentals, cyclical forces and macroeconomic policy have combined to slam the brakes on growth. China is making the last transition to a market economy: restructuring the state banks and state firms in order to place the economy on a sustainable growth path. If successful, these reforms will be beneficial in the long run, but in the short run they are highly disruptive. This is not to say that China will plunge into a crisis that will derail it for the next five or ten years. Chinese long-term economic prospects remain very good.

The authorities had the chance to avoid a hard landing and alleviate global financial imbalances, but they missed it. China should have let its currency appreciate as the boom progressed.

Both China and the rest of the world would have benefited. China would have increased the welfare of its people and avoided overheating the economy and creating excesses of resource misallocation. But the authorities always maintained that they would move in their own time, step by step. In July 2005 the government revalued the yuan against the dollar by 2% and introduced a more flexible regime. However, the central bank continued to intervene, in effect maintaining the new peg. The result is mounting upward pressure on the yuan as the current-account surplus is exploding, while speculators are finding new ways to penetrate the anyway porous capital controls. The Chinese authorities are faced with the choice between possible severe import quotas imposed by the US, and quite likely Europe, and a significant currency appreciation. A yuan revaluation seems the more likely outcome. Import restrictions, once imposed, could be difficult to change and would introduce an artificial distortion of trade. Over the medium term China could live with a stronger currency, but current wafer-thin profit margins leave firms extremely exposed to a jump in the exchange rate.

Economic fundamentals exacerbate the cycle: the role of the banking system

China is still a developing economy, which needs a lot of investment, especially in real estate and infrastructure. There is inherent strong demand for more housing. Property rights are better defined now and there has been an important shift to private housing in

Chinese cities. The process of urbanisation is far from complete. A lot more investment in infrastructure is needed, especially if the hinterland is to be opened up to benefit fully from buoyant economic activity. However, China needs efficient investment. With the banking system in state hands this has not been the case.

China has a huge domestic savings rate at 45–50% of GDP. The economy has its own funds to finance its need for fast capital accumulation. But China's banking system is dominated by four big state-owned banks, which account for two-thirds of domestic assets. Two-thirds of their lending goes to state-owned firms and local governments. Moribund state firms have been kept on life support as a sort of surrogate social security system. Private firms have little access to bank credit. The private business sector still relies mainly on retained earnings and FDI, with retained earnings being the more important source. Before 1998 the state banks did not lend to the household sector. The stock of household lending is still only 10% of total lending. Private banks have a tiny share of the market, and the rest is in the hands of credit co-operatives.

As a result, the bulk of bank lending is actually policy lending, not true lending in the market sense of the word. Moreover, most lending decisions are taken at the local branch level with little supervision from the government, making corruption rife. These loans are a direct, although hidden, liability of the government. The change in these liabilities should be included in the budget deficit. Figure 16 shows the budget deficit, adjusted for the annual change in banks' lending, which can be counted as policy lending. The series is far from perfect as the information is scant. But it

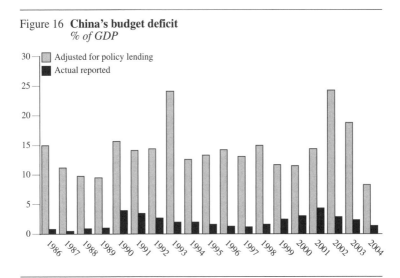

Figure 16 **China's budget deficit**
        % of GDP

does give a feel for the true size of the fiscal expansion during the boom years. The adjusted deficit was a record 24.3% of GDP in 2002 and 20% in 2003, compared with 24.1% of GDP in 1993 when inflation became rampant. The high inflation bout in 1993–95 was primarily driven by monetising the surging budget deficit. Since 1994, central bank lending directly to the government has been prohibited.

Cheap money leads to overinvestment

The consequence of cheap money in this system is an investment rate that reached 43% of GDP in 2004, up from a low of 34% in 1997. The increase in the share of investment in output during

1997–2004 was almost the same as during the crisis period of 1990–94. Domestic credit tells the same story. Domestic credit was 168% of GDP in 2004, up from 91% of GDP in 1995. In the past nine years this ratio increased at a much faster pace than in the previous 18 years. Moreover, it is one of the highest, if not the highest, in the world. For comparison, in the United States it is 90% of GDP and in Japan it is 140% of GDP.

It is not difficult to explain why this ratio is so high in China. The Chinese save a lot. Capital controls prevent them from investing abroad and so the savings stay at home. The state banks have implicit state guarantees and there are not many other places where the Chinese can keep their savings.

Figure 17 shows the change in domestic credit as a share of nominal GDP. It shot up to a record of nearly 40% of GDP in 2002 from 13% in 2000. It fell back to 30% in 2003, but it is difficult to imagine that all this credit has found productive uses.

The book *Mr China*[6] offers a poignant description of China's businessmen. It is a true story about the travails of a Wall Street banker, an ex-Red Guard and a Mandarin-speaking Englishman who invested $400 million in factories across China in the early and mid-1990s. It describes the behavioural patterns that the Chinese system encourages. The entrepreneurial managers react quickly, but they do not think about the big picture. Their focus is entirely on the short term. When there is a shortage of some kind, factories are built fast, usually creating a glut which ruins many of them. Chinese firms seem to exploit arbitrage opportunities with no regard for strategic planning. The book

Figure 17 **Change in domestic credit**
Share of nominal GDP, %

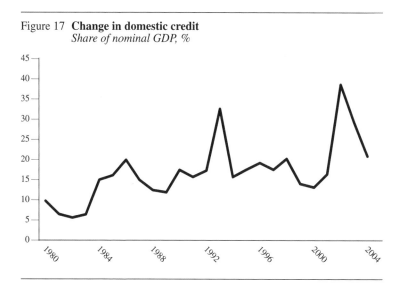

suggests that one explanation could be the inordinate amount of change and uncertainty that Chinese society has faced in its recent history, especially during the Cultural Revolution. These psychological dynamics and the inefficient banking system result in overinvestment.

Overinvestment increases cyclical volatility

Investment is the most volatile component of output. Therefore the huge investment to output ratio results in sharp cyclical swings. China has a dual economy, with a state side and a market side. On the market side, the investment accelerator principle bodes ill for capital expenditure in the coming years. The theory of the investment accelerator states that the change in investment is a function of the change in the growth of demand. If output growth stays the same in one year, in the next year there should be hardly any need for investment growth. If output growth slows, investment in the next year should fall. Because investment is such a large share of output, a shift from rapid growth to cuts in investment could shave a few percentage points off growth, even before accounting for the negative effects of weaker income on the rest of the economy.

In more detail, the theory of the investment accelerator is as follows. For an economy there is an optimal capital stock. It depends negatively on the expected effectiveness of technology. Improvement in technology means more output can be produced with less capital. It depends negatively on the real interest rate. Investment is made for two reasons: to bring capital to its desired level and to make up for capital lost through depreciation. The optimal capital stock is proportional to the expected output level, which can be justified both theoretically and empirically. The capital to output ratio is stable in the long run. GDP growth fluctuations are therefore associated with larger movements in investment. Investment is more volatile than output because it is based on expectations of the future.

If expectations remain high despite an observed slowdown, the investment accelerator principle will not work. This is rarely the case, but the likelihood is greater in China than anywhere else in the world. The reason is that FDI plays a big role in supplying the funds for investment in the private sector. Optimism among foreign investors who are pursuing the 'China growth story' could still remain buoyant at a time when domestic investors are scaling back their expectations. Foreign firms seem to want to be in China for the long run, never mind the occasional bumps. There is also a lot of pressure for company executives to show that they are in China, planning for the future.

That said, although FDI was important as a source of finance at the beginning of China's opening up, now it is much less so. Moreover, more than half of it has been recycled Chinese reinvested earnings. According to national statistics data, retained earnings accounted for 73% of the investment in fixed assets in 2004 and foreign funds for 4%. Because of the specific classification, this understates the true importance of FDI. According to IMF data, FDI accounted for 6% of fixed asset investment in 2004, down from 16% in 1994. The effect of the investment accelerator principle may be somewhat muted, but it is still likely to be a major force. However, if FDI collapses this will pose a serious threat in the medium term, as it is still important as a source of know-how. If China slows down significantly, with existing investment losses denting company profits outside China, it will be increasingly difficult for foreign investors not to lose their enthusiasm about China.

Current investment rate is unsustainable

The investment rate of 43% of GDP in 2004 is clearly unsustainable.[7] Assume that China's long-term real GDP growth rate is 8–9%. The shares of profits and wages in developed economies are generally stable over the long term, with the ratio usually being 40–60%. Hence, if GDP is 100, from the annual increment of 9, say 4 goes to earnings before interest, taxes, depreciation and amortisation. But this means a gross return on capital of 8%. With depreciation typically around 7–8%, this leaves nothing for net return on capital.

If the investment rate has to come down to its 25-year average of 33% of GDP, then China needs a cut of 10 percentage points to get there from where it was in 2004, say over the next five years. This is not consistent with a soft landing, i.e. nominal output growth moderating to around 9–10%. Let's say output growth is 10% a year in the next five years and at the end the investment ratio is 33%. This means that investment has to grow on average by about 1.5% a year, compared with about 20% during the boom years. It is this type of arithmetic that underlies the natural violence of the economic cycles that developing countries experience when growth is rapid.

South Korea's financial system of the 1960s and 1970s had much in common with China today, and the Korean experience provides valuable insight into the behaviour of an economy with cheap credit rationed by the government. South Korea's potential real growth rate averaged around 8.5% in the 1960s and 1970s, about the same as the estimated trend growth rate of China today. But the cyclical swings that the Korean economy went through were violent. The change of output growth from peak to trough averaged around 15 percentage points. In China we could only compare the change in real output growth over the past 25 years using annual data. The swings of real output growth averaged

6 percentage points before 1998. The nominal data show larger cyclical swings.[7]

Throughout the 1960s and 1970s, the Korean government used its financial institutions, especially the banks, to direct credit at low rates to strategic industries. By the early 1980s, it had become clear that several of the favoured sectors had performed badly, leaving banks with significant bad loans. Policy loans resulted in excessive investment, reaching 37% of output in 1979, up from 27% in 1976. Meanwhile, the economy was also overheating. Between the first quarter of 1979 and the fourth quarter of 1980, Korean output growth had collapsed by 18 percentage points.

Overheating has spurred a cyclical slowdown

On the state side of the economy the political cycle rules. The surge of investment since 2000 was the authorities' response to the global slowdown. This time round they do not have that option. China has already overheated. Overheating can coexist with overinvestment because of the different lead times of investment and the lack of market principles applied to certain investment decisions. There is overinvestment in the sectors where the factories could be built fast. There is overheating in sectors where it takes a few years to build the necessary capacity and where investment is directed by the planning authorities.

According to the consumer price index, data inflation has not been the problem it was in the 1993–94 period.[8] But this does not mean that the economy has not overheated. In a market economy, price fluctuations are the key mechanism to distribute scarce resources. But in China, the authorities regulate the price of energy, and energy is the primary input in virtually everything we produce. They have been raising energy prices, but with a substantial lag, not across the board and not enough to reflect the huge increase of energy prices on world markets. State oil refineries took the hit, buying some of the oil at world market prices and selling it at a lower price domestically. The duality of China's economy has made oil demand very elastic. The state oil refineries increasingly operate in the market side of the economy and are expected to maximise profits. But administered oil prices mean that in this system their profit-maximising strategy is to buy and process less oil.

The overheating in China has taken the form of severe shortages of energy, raw materials and transport. These shortages are the consequence of years of underinvestment. Investment in energy, transport and mining as a share of total investment has fallen continuously since 2000. Investment in these sectors is directed by the authorities. With an increasingly complex and more market-driven economy, it is no surprise that they have misjudged the need for infrastructure investment.

Infrastructure investment is subject to long lead times. Officials forecast that the energy shortages are unlikely to last beyond 2006. China has been pushing ahead with the construction of power plants, including for nuclear energy, in an attempt to provide the necessary new supply. The proponents of a soft landing have argued that the boost to infrastructure investment, planned for 2005 and 2006, will substitute for the investment boom in manufacturing and real estate and keep the economy growing fast.

But in December 2004 the state-owned newspaper *China Daily* reported:

> *China will step up controls on investment in power plants, despite electricity shortages, to help ease pressure on coal supplies.*

In January 2005 the *Wall Street Journal* wrote:

> *In an unusual display of regulatory bite, China's environmental watchdog has ordered a raft of partly built power plants valued at billions of dollars to suspend construction because they failed to file required paperwork. The move dovetails with Beijing's efforts to cool the overheated power industry and ease sharp demand for energy resources such as coal.*

Investment in energy supply is in itself one of the most energy-intensive types of investment, notwithstanding the severe environmental constraints China is already facing.

Domestic demand 'hard landing' already under way

The authorities recognised the problem of overinvestment and introduced administrative measures to restrain it and achieve a soft landing. Shortages and macroeconomic policy induced a cyclical slowdown, which began in the middle of 2004. China does not publish quarterly data on the level of real GDP or the components and, as mentioned earlier, the real annual GDP growth number is unreliable. Analysing the nominal GDP data seems much more indicative and trustworthy. China's expansion peaked at nominal growth rates of 18% in the middle of 2004. Output growth has come down since then, reaching 13% in the third quarter of 2005. At these rates nominal growth is close to its trend of 11%, but its composition continues to point to much weaker domestic demand. Domestic demand growth slowed to single digits in the first half of 2005 from double-digit growth rates in the previous two years.

The levelling off of imports, a big chunk of which is for investment, points to capital expenditure having faltered. The Chinese also publish a monthly series for fixed asset investment, according to which investment growth remains robust and has even accelerated. But this cannot be squared with other indicators, which show that firms are starved of finance. Bank credit is the biggest source of funds. Annual credit growth plummeted from 28% in mid-2003 to 1% in mid-2005, after a mild upswing in the first half of 2004. Another source of finance is FDI, which has levelled off since the start of 2005.

Firms could also use retained earnings. But overinvestment combined with overheating has squeezed profit margins from the top and from the bottom. From the top, profit margins have been eaten away by output price deflation, resulting from unfair competition and excess capacity. From the bottom, profits have been

Figure 18 **China: non-financial credit expansion**
Latest month on 6 months earlier, s.a.a.r., %

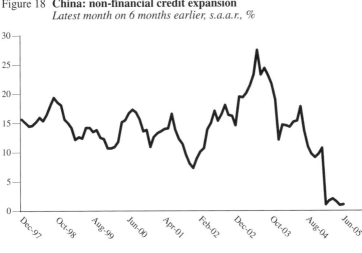

hurt by input price inflation from excess demand for commodities or physical shortages. Profit data are unreliable, but anecdotal evidence is not encouraging. Moreover, the National Bureau of Statistics conducted a survey of 200,000 companies in the manu-facturing sector and found that their losses in the seven months to July 2005 were 56% higher than in the same period a year earlier and already close to the loss for the whole of 2004.

External demand will falter, but consumers cannot take up the baton

Foreign demand has provided a key impetus to output growth in China. In 2004 the contribution from export growth was the same as the contribution from increased investment. China managed to dodge the global economic cycle in 2000–01 when it boosted investment in response to the bursting of the bubble in the United States. Rapid export growth has continued to keep the economy afloat after domestic demand weakened. Buoyant export income has also boosted consumer spending.

But in 2006 the US economy is likely to slow down significantly. Moreover, American consumers are likely to be the chief drag on growth. The contribution of Chinese export growth to Chinese output growth could almost halve. At present Chinese policymakers do not have the domestic ammunition they had in 2000.

Chinese consumers are left with the task of supporting the economy. While nominal investment and export growth exploded in the four years to 2004, up by 17% and 21% on average, consumer spending growth stayed relatively stable at an average rate of 8%. As a share of output, consumer spending fell to below its 1997 level. Consumer spending was never a growth driver, and it is too early to expect it could be an autonomous source of growth.

Real income is likely to be hurt by an investment meltdown and weakening export income and/or higher inflation. The authorities could ease fiscal policy in order to boost consumer incomes. They are considering an income tax cut, but given the lack of a social security safety net and fast-rising medical and education costs, the Chinese may decide to save rather than spend. One of the current priorities of the Communist Party is to bridge the urban–rural divide and redistribute income towards the rural areas. Creating a system that provides both rural and urban residents with higher security with respect to their health and their retirement will invariably be highly beneficial in spurring consumer spending and lowering the savings rate. But this will be a medium- to long-term process, which is unlikely to provide a cushion during the current cycle.

There is no scope for credit-driven consumer spending because of the weakness of the banking system. Household credit has doubled every year since 1998, but it is still only a small fraction of total credit. Banks have a lot to learn in order to be able to assess credit risk properly. The authorities should be stimulating household loans. Instead they introduced lending restrictions and regulations on household loans when it transpired that a big chunk of the existing household loans was already bad. There is a huge pent-up demand for housing, but at present the banking system cannot rise to the challenge. Consumer spending growth could accelerate, but this is unlikely given the multiplier effects. And even if it does, it will not be strong enough to outweigh a major drag from slower exports and capital expenditure.

The last transition to market economy

The banking system is the principal weak link in China. The authorities have realised this and have been moving fast to restructure it. All their efforts are textbook examples of the right things to do, but the task of successfully reforming the system is enormous. The authorities are unlikely to succeed without experiencing significant disruptions in the short term. After the Banking Regulatory Commission said in early 2005 that bank managers who were found to have authorised loans which then turned bad would be severely punished, it would not be a surprise if bankers lost their enthusiasm to lend at all. Moreover, they simply do not have the skills to be able to assess credit risk properly.

The whole of China's financial system is generally under-developed and reform of the non-bank financial sector is also needed. Although there has been progress on the capital markets front, private firms still have limited options for raising finance. The stockmarket continues to operate like a secret club for the state behemoths, providing further life-support for the zombies among them. Creating a market-based financial system, especially a transparent and well-run stockmarket, is crucial if China is to enter the next growth phase where proper profit-maximising incentives lead to the efficient distribution of domestic savings.

China is slowing down not only as a result of cyclical forces, reinforced by structural factors. It is also going through its next big phase of transition to a market economy – a transition which involves painful reforms of the financial sector, state firms and the rural sector.

Long-term growth constraints

Chinese economic dominance may be inevitable, but much further down the road. China has recently embarked on a spending spree abroad, leading some to conclude that the economy is rising at a pace to rival America. But the recent rush to acquire strategic foreign assets is far from being an expression of rising power: it is a testament to the tangible constraints that the economy faces. China's National Offshore Oil Corporation's (CNOOC) offer for Unocal, which the US Congress rejected, is a perfect example.

Over the past couple of years the Chinese authorities have been on a quest to acquire strategic energy resources throughout the world to secure future supply. In the battle for raw materials, China and America are outright rivals and future tensions are likely to increase. China's economic expansion involves an intensive use of raw materials. It is the most important economy in terms of incremental demand for energy and most other resources. In the boom years since 2000, China alone accounted for one-third of the incremental demand for oil, causing oil prices to more than double. But in current foreign exchange terms, China's economy is still much smaller than America's. When it comes to who can afford energy at high prices the United States is currently the clear winner.

Energy is a key constraint, in both the short term and in the long term. The long-term strategy of trying to secure future supply by gaining control of foreign resource assets is foolish and uneconomical. There is nothing to stop foreign governments from nationalising these companies. The recent Bolivian experience emphasises this point. The fact that the value of CNOOC is not much higher than the bid it put in for Unocal either shows pure desperation or an arriviste attitude, neither of which reveals economic muscle or shrewdness.

The same is true for most of the other types of acquisition

deals that Chinese firms have struck recently. Manufacturers such as Lenovo and TCL are buying western manufacturing firms in order to acquire brand names and sales networks. But they have done so on unfavourable terms. Their current scramble to position themselves globally is a consequence of poor strategic planning rather than an example of champions powering ahead.

To change business-sector attitudes, it may not be enough to improve the financial system by introducing market incentives. There are powerful psychological factors, related to the legacy of the communist regime that was alluded to above. As long as the Communist Party is in power, the short-termism that plagues business decisions may persist. Households also need to change. The banking system is insolvent but liquid. There have not been any major runs on the banks. Households have faith in the banking system because it is state owned, but for the same reason they do not feel responsible for repaying their loans. After all, the banks are perceived to be the people's banks. The authorities could face a counter-intuitive dilemma. Changing banks' lending practices may harm household confidence in the banking system, which could bring about its collapse. In the long run, liberal economics could clash with the rigid politics one way or another. The damage from possible political upheaval could be huge.

Another long-term obstacle on the road to dominance is the shortage of skilled labour. The banking sector is already experiencing a severe lack of qualified employees. On the face of it, China seems to have unlimited supply of cheap labour. Half of its labour force is still employed in rural areas. Urbanisation has been one of the main sources of fast growth in the economy, although the strain on infrastructure and social conditions has been enormous. The process of urbanisation will continue, but at some stage the quality of the labour force begins to matter more than the quantity. Because of its size, China has already become the global manufacturing base for certain products. For example, it has the capacity to supply nearly 80% of world demand for air conditioners and mobile phones. To move up the value-added manufacturing chain and also into services, China will need a much better educated labour force. In addition, with one of the government's current priorities being to bridge the rural–urban divide, it will become increasingly difficult for the manufacturing sector to find even cheap unskilled labour. Wages will have to rise and workers will have to be treated better. Higher wages could only be beneficial in the long term, as China needs to move away from investment-led growth to a consumer-driven expansion.

Significant yuan revaluation unavoidable

China has been growing much faster than its trading partners. Its balance-of-payments surplus has ballooned and it continues to expand its world market share. In the long run, its real exchange rate should be appreciating. This could be realised through higher inflation or nominal appreciation or a combination of both. The authorities devalued the yuan in 1994 after inflation spiralled out of control and then pegged it to the dollar. The real effective exchange rate did appreciate, which happened through weaker currencies of China's main trading partners against the US dollar.

Since the Asian crisis, China's neighbours, which account for 40% of its trade, have been pursuing cheap currency policies. But in early 2002 the situation reversed. The US dollar started to fall, and the yuan went down with it.

The lack of an exchange rate adjustment through the boom years and state interference to absorb inflationary pressures has prolonged China's super-competitive gorging on more and more of the world demand pie. The authorities had the chance to avoid a hard landing and alleviate global financial imbalances, but they missed it. They should have let the currency appreciate as the economy powered ahead. This would have increased the welfare of the population and avoided overheating the economy and creating excesses of resource misallocation. Their mercantilist attitude, reinforced by the Asian financial crisis, prevented them from seeing the benefits to the economy. They have too much faith in their ability to manage the domestic economy as long as external influences are, in their mind, kept at bay through the fixed exchange rate – this is now set to backfire. In a more general sense, the Chinese authorities have not caught up with the ascent of China's economy and its global reach. Setting policy by only looking inward and fumbling their way in the outside world bodes ill for the future management of China's economy, despite the success of its gradual policy approach so far.

The authorities have valued stability above all and have always maintained that they would change the exchange rate regime gradually in their own time. In July 2005 they revalued the yuan against the dollar by 2% and introduced a more flexible regime. However, the central bank continued to intervene, in effect main-

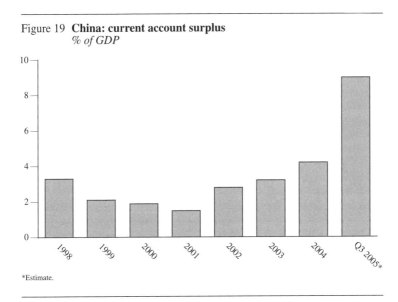

Figure 19 **China: current account surplus**
% of GDP

*Estimate.

taining a new peg. The result is mounting upward pressure on the yuan. Trade data for the first three quarters of 2005 reveal China's gigantic crowding out of the rest of the world. Its current-account surplus ballooned to 9% of GDP in the third quarter of 2005.

The Chinese authorities are faced with a choice between possible severe import quotas imposed by America, and quite likely Europe, and a significant currency appreciation. A yuan revaluation seems the more likely outcome. Import restrictions, once imposed, could be difficult to change and would introduce an artificial distortion of trade. China could deal with a stronger yuan in the medium term, but the current precarious state of business profitability leaves the economy vulnerable to an exchange rate shock in the short term.

Conclusion

The interaction between the planned and market side of China's economy has always resulted in booms followed by busts. During each boom lax monetary policy, channelled through a state-owned banking system, leads to overinvestment on a massive scale. Profit-maximising principles do not guide investment decisions. As in Japan during the 1970s and 1980s, the focus is on stakeholder value or, even worse, on arbitrage opportunities. When the economy overheats, excess capacity exacerbates the cyclically induced slowdown. The domestic demand hard landing is already under way, but exports, the economy's growth engine, are still powering ahead. With American demand likely to weaken significantly in 2006, the last support to growth could buckle.

The violent nature of the Chinese cycle has not changed, but the economy has expanded tremendously to affect the world economy. China has been a global locomotive during the past few years, but since mid-2004 its voracious expansion has been at the expense of the rest of the world. The beginning of the work-out of China's domestic imbalances – the huge overinvestment – has put tremendous pressure on the global economy. The next few years are likely to be crucial for China's economy, putting to the test the authorities' resolve to make the last transition to a market economy. Welcoming the benign force of foreign competition has already made China a much more likely candidate for eventual global dominance than Japan ever was. Should the Chinese push ahead with the remaining hard reforms, bar any political troubles, the economy should continue to realise its vast potential for catch-up growth.

Notes

1 Lombard Street Research's *Monthly International Review (MIR)* no. 143, September 2004: 'US balance sheets serially trashed by Eurasian surplus', Charles Dumas. Dr Bernanke's speech was given on 10 March 2005.

2 Lombard Street Research's *MIR* no. 122, November 2002: 'Emerging Eurasia to dominate world economy by 2025', Charles Dumas.

3 Lombard Street Research's *MIR* no. 97, July 2000: 'US corporate profits: sharp fall likely in 2001–02. E-dementia misallocates resources – www hitting USA.com and USA Inc', Charles Dumas.

4 see note 2.

5 Lombard Street Research's *MIR* no. 144, October 2004, 'China heads for a hard landing', Diana Choyleva.

6 *Mr China* by Tim Clissold, 2004, Constable & Robinson.

7 Recent unofficial comments from the Chinese Statistical Bureau have alluded to the annual real GDP growth number being unreliable and only confirmed our conviction that nominal GDP data are more trustworthy. You can count money GDP, but you have to calculate real GDP. The recent upward restatement of China's 2004 nominal GDP affects very little the analysis of saving and investment excesses in this book and (so far) leaves growth rates unchanged.

8 The CPI data are also problematic. The Chinese authorities claim that 95% of all prices are deregulated, but they still fiddle with the rest. In early 2005, the Chinese planning body issued a statement to local governments to freeze the prices of those items in the CPI that have seen monthly increases of more than 1%.

Index